"Before reading this book, I thought that everything that needs to be said about biblical forgiveness had already been said. I was wrong. What makes this book unique is how Brad goes beyond the basics to dig deeply into the struggles and the questions we all face when being called upon to forgive those who have hurt us. Brad draws from his extensive counseling experience to address almost every imaginable situation and to correct common misunderstandings. I also appreciate the high regard he shows for Scripture as he offers wise answers to important questions."

Jim Newheiser, Director of the Christian Counseling Program and Associate Professor of Pastoral Theology, Reformed Theological Seminary; executive director, The Institute for Biblical Counseling and Discipleship (IBCD); author of *Money, Debt, and Finances*

"Brad Hambrick has done the body of Christ a much-needed favor by addressing the topic and practice of forgiveness with thoughtful nuance to the realities of trauma and abuse. His tone and empathy will be welcome words to those who have had forgiveness required of them in ways that are harmful and unwise. As he clears the debris of unhelpful notions of forgiveness, he paves the way for a robust, redemptive path to forgiving."

Timothy S. Lane, President, Institute for Pastoral Care and Tim Lane & Associates

"*Making Sense of Forgiveness* is a one-of-a-kind, comprehensive resource that addresses both the common and complex matters of forgiveness. With expert clarity and theological accuracy, Brad explores the many spiritual, personal, and relational implications of forgiveness while sensitively taking into account the various and unique circumstances that can confuse the process. It is a healing approach to forgiveness that is sure to help many people."

Eliza Huie, LCPC, Director of Counseling at McLean Bible Church, Vienna, VA; author of *Raising Kids in a Screen-Saturated World*, *Raising Kids in a Hyper-Sexualized World*, and coauthor of *The Whole Life*

"*Making Sense of Forgiveness* helps readers consider often overlooked but essential aspects of forgiveness. Brad's eye-opening insights are critical for those who are committed to preserving unity within the body of Christ, restoring broken relationships, and helping others understand how to forgive as they've been forgiven by our Lord."

Sam Hodges IV, Vice President of Publishing, Church Initiative

"The practice of forgiveness is central to life as a disciple of Jesus Christ. But it is not easy, nor is it always clear how to proceed. Brad Hambrick is a trustworthy shepherd who leads us carefully through a nuanced and practical discussion of this complex topic. Whether you are a person who has been sinned against and are wrestling with forgiving the one who hurt you or an offender receiving forgiveness from the one you hurt, Brad's biblically-saturated guide will help you take the next wise step."

Michael R. Emlet, Dean of Faculty and counselor, Christian Counseling & Educational Foundation (CCEF); author of *Saints, Sufferers, and Sinners: Loving Others as God Loves Us*

"Extending and receiving forgiveness is sometimes like a sprint. More often it is like a marathon. Running well and finishing the race requires a well-planned strategy. It also is significantly aided by helpful companions. This book is one such companion. It is a reservoir of biblical wisdom. I cannot commend it more highly."

Daniel L. Akin, President, Southeastern Baptist Theological Seminary

"There are few voices I trust more than Brad Hambrick. This is especially true as he navigates us through the deep and often tumultuous terrain of forgiveness. From the suffering saint to the seasoned counselor, anyone who reads this book will immediately benefit from its rich teaching on a most important topic. I can say confidently that this will be a resource I will turn to with frequency and joy. I trust the same for all who read it."

Jonathan D. Holmes, Executive Director, Fieldstone Counseling; pastor of counseling, Parkside Church

MAKING SENSE OF FORGIVENESS

MAKING SENSE OF
FORGIVENESS
MOVING FROM HURT TOWARD HOPE

Brad Hambrick

New
Growth
Press
newgrowthpress.com

New Growth Press, Greensboro, NC 27401
newgrowthpress.com
Copyright © 2021 by Brad Hambrick

Cover Design: Matt Naylor, mattnaylor.com
Interior Design and Typesetting: Gretchen Logterman

ISBN: 978-1-64507-143-3 (Print)
ISBN: 978-1-64507-144-0 (eBook)

Library of Congress Cataloging-in-Publication Data

Names: Hambrick, Brad, 1977- author.
Title: Making sense of forgiveness : moving from hurt toward hope / Brad
   Hambrick.
Description: Greensboro, NC : New Growth Press, [2021] | Summary: "Pastor
   and counselor Brad Hambrick helps readers who feel stuck to understand
   forgiveness as the start of a journey that doesn't erase the past, but
   honestly confronts hurt and clears the way for a hope-filled discussion
   on how to move toward healing"-- Provided by publisher.
Identifiers: LCCN 2021008601 (print) | LCCN 2021008602 (ebook) | ISBN
   9781645071433 (trade paperback) | ISBN 9781645071440 (ebook)
Subjects: LCSH: Forgiveness--Religious aspects--Christianity. |
   Interpersonal relations--Religious aspects--Christianity.
Classification: LCC BV4647.F55 H3545 2021 (print) | LCC BV4647.F55
   (ebook) | DDC 234/.5--dc23
LC record available at https://lccn.loc.gov/2021008601
LC ebook record available at https://lccn.loc.gov/2021008602

Printed in the United States of America

28 27 26 25 24 23 22 21   1 2 3 4 5

CONTENTS

Section 4: Embracing Forgiveness from Others

March

Section 5: Moving toward What Is Commonly Called "Closure"

April

Section 6: Avoiding Ministry Mishaps

May

Foreword

"I choose to let go. . . .
I choose to trust God's justice. . . .
I choose to leave it in God's hands. . . .
I choose to forgive. . . .

I closed the folder I'd stashed my loose-leaf journal in.
I felt better.
I'd handled it.
I was fine. Two days later, I realized . . . it wasn't that easy."[1]

The day I wrote those words in my journal—as a teenager wrestling through sexual abuse I was just beginning to understand—was the day I took a step I knew had to be taken. Somehow, I had to loosen the hold my abuser had over me. I was desperate to find a way to cut the ties and desperate to be the good Christian girl who responded the "right way." I carried the guilt of my abuse, and I didn't want to fail again. I'd been taught that forgiveness was both a command and a necessity—something I must do, something I would *need* to do, for my own healing.

---

1. Rachael Denhollander, *What Is a Girl Worth?: My Story of Breaking the Silence and Exposing the Truth about Larry Nassar and USA Gymnastics* (Carol Stream: Tyndale Momentum, 2019), 88.

Not knowing where to begin my journey or how to heal, I made a list of the things I could choose. I couldn't choose what had been done to me, but forgiveness—my response to abuse—was within my power. So through anger and tears, I chose. That night, I felt the relief I'd been promised. I meant the words I had written, and their sincerity brought conviction that I had won a hard-fought battle (you'll read about this step, crisis forgiveness, as you walk through this book). What I did not know that night was that this choice wasn't the end but rather the beginning: the beginning of a multi-year journey to discover what forgiveness really meant, and why in fact it was so critical. I didn't know in that moment that the exhausted relief was nothing more than a brief calm before the storm. Not forty-eight hours later I was reeling, beginning to realize that what I thought was the closing of a door was really the wedge that allowed it to burst open.

You see, in order to truly forgive, I had to first acknowledge the reality of the wound. That meant memories. It meant admitting damage when I wanted to be whole. Not being whole meant weakness and vulnerability. And vulnerability was what brought the abuse in the first place.

It also meant deep wrestling with the theology and practical reality of forgiveness. Far from any Hallmark movie portrayal, "I forgive you" wasn't the magic phrase that brought healing and a tearful reconciliation between the wounded and the wounder. My declaration of forgiveness was met with silence (and years later, with predictable and continued denial). There was no beautiful, redemptive story of relationship restored after I penned those words.

And, it meant making myself vulnerable to each and every way forgiveness is weaponized against the wounded. I had seen Christians do it so many times before—"I'm sure that was hard but . . . look at all the beauty that came from it!" as if the gaping wound and painful scar no longer mattered, or worse, didn't exist at all. Christians love happy endings, and "forgiveness" was far too often treated like a glittery bow topping off the perfectly wrapped "package" of a Christian "witness," used to minimize the depth of evil that has been done—or to minimize the reality that, this side of heaven, full healing doesn't come. What's hiding under the sparkling bow is often treated as much less important, as long as the package shimmers enough. I didn't need to hand anyone one more excuse to minimize and downplay the damage of abuse.

I'd seen forgiveness weaponized to pressure wounded people into unsafe relationships, to remove consequences or justice from those who caused great harm, or leveraged in immediate response to a suffering person's appeal for help. Forgiveness was supposed to be beautiful and redemptive, but the flowery descriptions of this core theology of the Christian faith lacked much theological depth and seemed woefully ignorant of practical realities. It *wasn't* the powerful truth it was held out to be. Until . . . I actually understood it. And then it was.

The journey that I went on, in the years following the night I thought I was closing a door, is the same journey you will be invited on in this book. A journey that delves into what it truly means to forgive, and why this theological truth really is grounded in the person and work of our Redeemer, in the holiest and most beautiful of ways. With gentleness and sensitivity to the real suffering that has taken place whenever the question of forgiveness is raised, Brad lays out a concise and comprehensive approach to understanding forgiveness and what it entails. Much as I did, you will wrestle with what forgiveness is—and what it is not. You will consider the ways it has been weaponized or misunderstood, and contrast inaccurate ideas with deeper understanding of what Scripture really means when it commands us to forgive. You will grapple with the real need to forgive in your own healing journey and why forgiveness is integral to freedom, but also walk through understanding false repentance, manipulation, and the difference between forgiveness and restoration. With insightful reflection questions and practical steps to help wisely guide the process, Brad couples careful exegesis with day-to-day application, bringing clarity and direction to a critical concept too often mired in misunderstanding and unhelpful practices.

It isn't an easy journey, nor a fast journey. But it is a vital one. My prayer for you as you walk through the material in this book, gently and as you are ready, is that you also will find rest for your soul and freedom in the truth of what it means to forgive, and be forgiven.

Rachael Denhollander
Speaker, Author, Victim Advocate

Introduction

A GUIDE TO THE JOURNEY AHEAD

Forgiveness is a beautiful theme for a redemptive novel or movie. We enjoy crying sweet tears as we watch. But as a lived experience, forgiveness means we've been hurt and are making ourselves vulnerable again. As C. S. Lewis famously wrote, "Everyone says forgiveness is a lovely idea until they have something to forgive."[1]

This book is written for those who are stuck on the difficult journey of forgiveness or for those who are walking alongside a friend who is stuck. For that reason, we won't view forgiveness as a lovely idea but, rather, as a hard journey. In reality, forgiveness is both beautiful *and* difficult.

The base metaphor we will use to define forgiveness is *canceling a debt*. Forgiveness means a loan of trust was given, which allowed us to be hurt. Whether we choose to extend another loan after canceling the debt is a matter of *trust* (another theme explored here), not forgiveness.

This book is written for those who are struggling to move forward on the road of forgiveness. It is not a memoir looking back from the end of the journey with all the luxuries hindsight affords.

1. C. S. Lewis, *Mere Christianity* (New York: Harper Collins, 2003), p. 115.

This book describes a process that is not "neat" because life in a broken world is not "tidy." Relationships are hard. Simplistic relational formulas only serve to discourage us as we strive to gain our bearings.

My aim in this book is to articulate what we often think but feel bad saying out loud. Our pain and confusion won't be resolved with silence, which only allows pain to echo. If we're going to find resolution, we have to be honest about what makes forgiveness hard.

Most important, forgiveness ultimately only makes sense in light of the death, burial, and resurrection of Jesus Christ. His sacrifice, rather than making forgiveness easy, is the foundation that can support the emotional weight of forgiveness.

No one can get far on the road of forgiveness without being vulnerable. Use this resource to invite a few friends with you along the way and help them understand what makes the terrain hard.

To be invited to walk alongside you and have your trust is an honor. I pray that what you read here will reward that trust. Thank you for allowing me to walk a piece of this journey with you.

Section 1:
Definitions and
Misunderstandings

We often resist hard things because we don't feel understood or because we don't understand what is (and isn't) required of us. We hesitate to talk to a friend because they haven't been through what we have. We pull back from accepting a new role because we're not sure what will be asked of us and we're afraid it will be too much. But pulling back doesn't make life easier; it makes life lonelier and heavier.

The goal of this first section is to remove obstacles to understanding the journey of forgiveness. If after reading it, you can say, "He gets it" or "I feel safe talking about why this is hard," then this first section has been a success. If you feel a sense of relief because misconceptions about forgiveness have been removed, that will be a significant step forward on your journey.

Chapter 1

REMEMBER, FORGIVENESS BEGINS WITH PAIN

Whena friend talks about needing to forgive someone, what do we know about them? We know they're hurting. Whatever journey God has for them will start with understanding their pain. When God was going to lead Israel out of Egypt, he said to Moses, "I have surely *seen the affliction* of my people who are in Egypt and have *heard their cry* because of their taskmasters. *I know their sufferings*" (Exodus 3:7, emphasis added).

God sees, God hears, and God knows. God repeats himself to emphasize the importance of being known when cultivating trust. If we don't take the time to understand, our friend will feel more like a problem to be solved than a person to be heard. Rushing to the remedy undermines trust. No one wants an orthodontist who promises to align their teeth in six weeks. The process would be too painful no matter how "right" the outcome.

EASY DOES IT

Often, we forget that good conversations begin where someone is rather than where they should be. When we're excited about the destination and rush the journey, we do not serve our friend well.

Forgiveness may be one of the subjects where Christians are most prone to rush one another.

Notice the connection between understanding and trust building portrayed in Hebrews 4:15–16:

> For we do not have a high priest [Jesus] who is unable to sympathize with our weaknesses, but one who in every respect has been tempted as we are, yet without sin. Let us then with confidence draw near to the throne of grace, that we may receive mercy and find grace to help in time of need.

Because Jesus deeply understands our life challenges—temptations and weaknesses—we are compelled to draw near to him with confidence. This is what it looks like to be "ambassadors for Christ" (2 Corinthians 5:20). We embody this priestly role of identifying with the pain of our friend in order to cultivate courage to take the steps ahead. Jesus built relational capital to cultivate trust and motivation. Our conversations about forgiveness should do the same. This occurs through compassionate questions and patient listening.[1]

If you are the person needing to forgive and yearn for someone to hear you, give someone you trust a copy of this chapter and ask, "Would you be this kind of friend for me?" Every journey is easier with a companion.

If you are the companion, here are some questions that could help you get to know where someone is on their forgiveness journey. Every situation is different, so some of the questions may be more or less relevant.

- *What happened?* Allow your friend to tell their story.

---

1. If you struggle to be a patient listener, consider my fifteen-minute video overview of good listening skills: "The Pastor as Counselor Lesson 4: Incarnational Ministry—Listening and Empathy," bradhambrick.com, January 28, 2020, http://bradhambrick.com/PastorAsCounselor4/.

- *What cultivated the trust that made this offense more hurtful?* Broken trust magnifies pain. Often pain is as much a function of the trust violated (think, gunpowder) as is the offense (think, fire). If we only assess the size and heat of the fire, we miss the point.

- *What is missing from your life as a result of the offense?* The consequences of an offense can be as disruptive as the primary offense itself. If we don't know the "dominos" of the offense, our friend is likely to feel like we just don't get it.

- *What other relationships are compromised because of the strain?* Our relationships tend to be like threads in a spider web. Changing one distorts the shape of the others.

- *What emotions do you cycle through as you deal with this offense?* Often anger gets all the attention when forgiveness is relevant. Don't neglect hearing fear, grief, confusion, and other relevant emotions.

- *What steps have you taken to make things better, and how did that go?* Talking to you is likely not the first proactive step they've taken. Before making suggestions, encourage them by affirming the wise things they've already done.

- *What steps are you considering?* Understanding what your friend thinks is next helps you get to know where they are on their journey.

- *Who else do you have supporting you, and how understood do you feel?* The less understood your friend feels, the more weight they will put on your relationship. You should be aware of this dynamic.

- *What question do you wish I'd ask?* This is an open-ended question to help make sure you're not missing something important.

Initially, the focus is on getting to know the person and their experience. This engagement builds trust and provides clarity about what other conversations may be helpful.

Notice what we did *not* ask first: "What log do you need to remove from your own eye?" (see Matthew 7:3–5). Is this an important question? Absolutely. Is it a first question? Usually not. Jesus's point in the Sermon on the Mount was twofold. First, when taking steps toward reconciliation, we need to model the kind of ownership of our personal failings we want the other person to display. Second, we have more control over our actions than another person's actions—hence, the difference in size between the log and speck.[2]

Notice, Jesus was *not* saying, (1) "Your actions are more important than the actions of the person who offended you," (2) "You are ready to take steps toward reconciliation," or (3) "The other person is ready for you to take steps towards reconciliation."[3] When we jump too quickly from our friend's anger to Matthew 7, we inadvertently put these words in Jesus's mouth.

When we listen well and build trust, we will arrive at Matthew 7 when it is a "word fitly spoken" (Proverbs 25:11). Like the punch line of a good joke, applicable counsel becomes less effective when it's given too soon.[4] If you are the person needing to forgive, and advice from well-intentioned friends (even advice you agreed with) was hard to receive, it may have been premature.

QUESTIONS FOR REFLECTION

1. Think of a time when you needed to forgive. How would it help you to have a friend hear you in the ways this chapter describes?

---

2. For more on how Matthew 7:1–6 applies to chronically broken relationships, see "Series: Marriage with a Chronically Self-Centered Spouse," bradhambrick.com, October 15, 2012 (particularly articles 3, 4, and 5), http://bradhambrick.com/selfcenteredspouse/.
3. If the relational offense is abusive, then reconciliation is not the next step. It is recommended that you consult https://churchcares.com for guidance on next steps based on the type of abuse that is involved.
4. If you are prone to arrive at needed advice prematurely (before your friend is ready for it), consider this brief reflection on the timing of truth in counseling: "On Counseling and Comedy," bradhambrick.com, July 13, 2013, http://bradhambrick.com/on-counseling-and-comedy/.

2. Can you think of times when you were willing to do what needed to be done next (whether forgiveness or another response) but feeling rushed created a sense of resistance within you? How did feeling rushed and misunderstood become a setback for you?

Chapter 2

FIVE THINGS
FORGIVENESS IS NOT

Initially, we paused to honor the pain that prompted the need to forgive. Now, we'll articulate several of the fears that can cause us to brace against forgiving.

Sometimes the most loving way to engage a subject is to set a sufferer's mind at ease. With children, this might sound like, "You've got a doctor's appointment today, but don't worry, you don't have to get any shots." It is reasonable to associate doctors with needles, but it easier to go to the doctor if you know there won't be any needles . . . at least, this time.

Similarly, it can be helpful to set our mind at ease by presenting five of the most common fears associated with forgiveness.

1. FORGIVENESS IS NOT PRETENDING I'M NOT HURT

If we conceive of forgiveness as pretending, then forgiveness becomes a synonym for being fake. Forgiveness becomes a form of self-imposed silencing. Loss of voice only compounds the painful effect of whatever offense has already been committed against us. Forgiveness is not pretending.

Simply stated—but simpler to say than to live—*forgiveness is what allows us to express hurt as hurt rather than hurt as anger.* Even after we forgive, hurt still hurts. If the person who hurt us gets upset with us for still hurting, they haven't really repented.

Too often we view forgiveness as the culmination of a journey. But when I say, "I forgive you," I am not saying, "Things are all better now." I am saying, "I have decided I will relate to your offense toward me differently." Forgiveness is the start of a new journey. Forgiveness does not erase the past.

When you forgive, you are not making a commitment not to feel hurt. You are making a commitment about what you will do with the hurt when it flares up.

2. FORGIVENESS IS NOT LETTING SOMEONE OFF THE HOOK

When we let someone off the hook, we are saying that nothing else needs to be done. It's the equivalent of someone eating your lunch out of the office fridge, and you saying, "That's okay, I needed to diet anyway." That is letting someone off the hook.

But when God forgives us, he does not assume we are a "finished product." God remains active in our life to remove the sin he forgave. *Forgiveness is meant to change us, not leave us as we were.* Similarly, when we forgive someone, it is right to expect that our grace toward them will have an impact on them. If someone does not agree about the wrongness of their sin and desire to change, then the most our forgiveness can do is set us free from bitterness. It would be unwise to restore the relationship to the same level of trust it had before.[1]

3. FORGIVENESS IS NOT MAKING AN EXCUSE FOR SOMEONE

Sometimes we resist forgiving because we do not want to ratify a perceived downgrade in the significance of the offense. Forgiveness

---

1. More will be said on the relationship between forgiveness, trust, and restoration in section 3 of this book; that is, chapters 9–15.

is not a downgrade. Forgiveness does not reclassify an offense from a "sin" to a "mistake." *Mistakes are excused. Sins are forgiven.*

Forgiveness inherently classifies an offense at the top level of wrongness. When we say, "I forgive you," we are saying, "The only thing that could make right what you did was Jesus's substitutionary death on the cross." For someone wanting to excuse their sin, real forgiveness is offensive (see 1 Corinthians 1:18–31).

4. FORGIVENESS IS NOT FORGETTING

We will devote chapters 7 and 16 to the misguided notion of "forgive and forget." Here we will merely seek to alleviate the fear that you will be pressured to forget. Most of us wish it were possible to forget our most painful experiences. Spiritual dementia toward our pain sounds blissful.

Forgiveness doesn't unwrite history. Jesus both cried out, "Father, forgive them, for they know not what they do" (Luke 23:34), and inspired the recording—the permanent remembering—of the events that led to his death. Forgiveness did not unwrite history or mitigate any of the benefits that come with learning from history. Whatever vulnerability true forgiveness brings, it is not the vulnerability of naivety.

So, what does forgiveness mean you are committing to do with your memories, fears, and imagination? Forgiveness does not add anything new to how you respond to your memories, fears, and imagination that wise relational practices would not have already entailed before you forgave.

We want to have a wise relationship with our memories.

- We want to mitigate the torment painful and intrusive memories caused.
- We want to learn any lessons about wise trust our painful memories can teach us.
- We want to prevent mistrust from spreading to other relationships.

Even if we are in a place we never wanted to find ourselves, we still want forgiveness to be part of what God does to contribute to our flourishing from here.

5. FORGIVENESS IS NOT NECESSARILY TRUST OR RECONCILIATION

You may remember geometry class in high school. You were taught "all squares are rectangles, but not all rectangles are squares." A similar relationship exists between forgiveness and trust or reconciliation: "All trust and reconciliation are rooted in forgiveness, but not all forgiveness results in trust and reconciliation."

When we don't realize this, we think saying, "I forgive you," implies things are "back to normal," and normal is what got us hurt. No thank you!

In chapters 13 and 14, we will consider when reconciliation is wise and what trust development looks like after a major offense. For now, all you need to realize is that the decision to forgive and the decision to trust are two different decisions. The first does not necessitate the second. If you are being pressured to believe that forgiving requires trusting, this is reason to push "pause" on trusting the person who is pressuring you.

QUESTIONS FOR REFLECTION *pretending I'm not hurt*

1. What fears about forgiveness did this chapter help you set aside? What experiences prompted these fears?
2. Review the sentence "For someone wanting to excuse their sin, real forgiveness is offensive." Does this statement help alleviate your fear that forgiveness minimizes what happened and allows the person who hurt you to "win"?

Chapter 3

THREE DIMENSIONS OF FORGIVENESS

When I say, "I forgive you," what am I committing to? This is the question we desperately want answered. We want to know what kind of check we are writing when we proclaim forgiveness over some hurtful action.

At its most basic level, forgiveness is canceling a debt. But to stay within the financial metaphor, canceling a debt doesn't necessarily mean living as if the debt never happened (rewriting history), giving another loan (trust), or starting a new business together (reconciliation). You can cancel a debt while being aware of someone's financial habits, declining to lend more money, and refusing another joint business venture.

For clarity, consider another question: What would it look like to hold an emotional-relational debt over someone? Whatever forgiveness means, it would be the opposite of the answer to this question. The answer for most situations can be summarized in the word *leverage*. We hold a debt against someone when we leverage their offense to coerce them into an action they do not voluntarily choose.

We will consider three ways offenses can be leveraged: (1) intrapersonally, (2) interpersonally, and (3) socially. Then we will consider how forgiveness leads us toward a different response.

1. INTRAPERSONAL IMPLICATIONS FOR FORGIVENESS

Intrapersonal means within (intra) ourselves (personal). We can leverage an offense against someone within our mind and attitudes. What does this look like? It looks like writing a narrative about this person that reduces them to their offense and evaluates the rest of their life through the lens of their offense.

The intrapersonal effects of forgiveness refer to the changes in your mind and emotions as a result of forgiving.

For instance, someone lies to us. Internally, we make them a flat character (a one-dimensional character like those in *Winnie the Pooh*, where Tigger is only an extrovert and Piglet is only a worrier). The offender is now a liar. They have no right to talk about honesty, integrity, justice, or virtue to anyone in any setting for any reason. For them to do so is disruptive to us because it conflicts with the character we've declared them to be.

This pattern of unforgiveness becomes more destructive when it generalizes to an entire population. The person who hurt us now represents all men, all women, all bosses, all members of a particular race, all member of a socioeconomic status, and so on.

An intrapersonal effect of forgiving is allowing someone to become a three-dimensional character—someone with multiple facets to their personhood, any of which may be most relevant to a given situation. Our friend who lied to us may be a great parent, teacher, or coach who is appreciated for their excellence in these roles. That can be true, and at the same time, they can still be a lousy friend whose lack of ownership for their sin against us makes it unwise for us to trust them.

This aspect of forgiveness protects us from being emotionally disrupted by every compliment this person receives and every accomplishment they achieve. We are liberated from being upset by good fortune in the life of someone who hurt us.

2. INTERPERSONAL IMPLICATIONS FOR FORGIVENESS

Interpersonal means between (inter) us and the person who offended us. We can leverage an offense against someone by the expectations we place on them or the special rules we expect to govern the relationship.

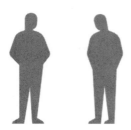

The interpersonal effects of forgiveness refer to changes in how you and the person who offended you relate to one another.

Returning to the example of the friend who lied to us, we could expect that they give deference to our preferences moving forward (expectations) or that they give tangible evidence that all their statements are true (special rules).

If our friend is unwilling to voluntarily offset their deceit with more forthrightness, there is reason to question their repentance. In that case, forgiveness should not progress toward trust. But if we try to force the fruit of repentance, we get baited into matching their lack of repentance with attempts to coerce change (leverage). We respond to one unhealthy pattern with a different unhealthy pattern of relating. That is not good for our soul, the other person, or the relationship.

Forgiving means not using past offenses as trump cards in present decision-making. When we forgive, we forgo the verbal formula "Because you did [sinful action], I expect you to [positive action]" or "Because you did [sinful action], you have no right to [otherwise reasonable action]."

This means we make requests rather than demands. So it would sound like, "It would help me if you would [positive action] because I'm still recovering from [sinful action]." If a reasonable request is made and is met with an aggressive, defensive, or neglectful response, the relationship is not at a point where trust and reconciliation are warranted.

3. SOCIAL IMPLICATIONS FOR FORGIVENESS

We can leverage an offense socially by speaking negatively of the person who hurt us in order to harm their reputation. This can be either top-of-mind-tip-of-tongue conversation or intentional conversation.

The social effects of forgiveness refer to the impact forgiving has on the relationships you share with the person who offended you.

Top-of-mind-tip-of-tongue conversation occurs when the pain is fresh, and everything reminds us of the offense. Often the person we're talking to feels like our disclosure of pain is a change of subject to the conversation. These conversations frequently occur before we've had time to process the pain or the person who hurt us has made an attempt to repent.

For instance, a shared friend of the person who lied to us may say, "I really don't like the tone they use when correcting their children," and we reply, "I know! Ever since they lied to me about [subject], I think everything they say is meant to be hurtful." We changed the subject from their parenting to our pain, and we brought an additional person into the original conflict.

Intentional conversation is usually something we intend to be a warning. Using our example of the friend who lied to us again, we talk to someone else who is interacting with that friend. We remember what happened and try to discern, "Is this person in danger of being lied to, or do I just want to create mistrust toward the person who hurt me?" Either answer may be accurate. The first would be protecting a mutual friend. The latter would be unforgiving toward the person who hurt me.

Socially, forgiving means refraining from tarnishing the reputation of the person who hurt us for reasons other than protecting others. (More will be said on protecting the vulnerable in chapter 26.) Even this statement is frustrating because it's not cut-and-dried. It requires wisdom to assess situations and self-awareness about our own motives. One of the things we'll have to wrestle with in this book is that forgiveness requires wisdom and cannot be reduced to rules.

To summarize, forgiveness means keeping three commitments:

1. *Intrapersonally*—I will not dwell on this offense and reduce you to this failure.
2. *Interpersonally*—I will not use this offense as leverage to coerce you to involuntarily change.
3. *Socially*—I will not bring up this event with others unless it is to protect them.

FORGIVE AS CHRIST FORGAVE YOU?

We now come to the biblical phrase about forgiveness that has the most power—meaning it can be used for both the greatest blessing and greatest harm: forgive as Christ forgave you (see Ephesians 4:32; Colossians 3:13). This is the phrase that can be used to flip forgiveness on the person who has been hurt and seems to imply unqualified restoration or blind vulnerability. But does it?

We'll wrestle with this phrase throughout this book, but for now consider the fact that not everyone goes to heaven (Matthew 7:21), and Jesus did not entrust himself to everyone (John 2:24). Jesus was exceedingly gracious but no doormat.[1] Jesus extends the opportunity for relationship, but he does not allow people with the intent to do harm to set the terms for the relationship. With Jesus there is nothing unforgivable, but there is not forgiveness on any terms.

When we read a simple statement like "God is not mocked" (Galatians 6:7), we often fail to recognize that this means God doesn't get conned by false tears, doesn't get manipulated by conflicts of interests, and doesn't wrestle his own emotional limitation. We do get caught in these binds. So, we seek to forgive as Christ forgave us amid these challenges. This requires wisdom.

QUESTIONS FOR REFLECTION

1. Which aspect of forgiveness is most difficult for you? Is that because the implications are cognitively unclear (i.e., confusing), emotionally difficult (i.e., upsetting), or relationally complicated (i.e., currently unclear)?

2. What is your response to the idea that "forgiving as Christ forgave you" requires wisdom to apply instead of just being a rule we can follow?

Can you forgive if you don't have peace about something?

---

1. For further study on this aspect of Jesus's relational life, consider Gary Thomas's book *When to Walk Away*, which is an examination of how Jesus responded to toxic people.

Chapter 4

THREE THINGS WE DON'T NEED TO FORGIVE

When talking about forgiveness, it can be easy to fall into the "to-a-man-with-a-hammer-everything-looks-like-a-nail" trap. We can get so excited about forgiveness that we start trying to forgive everything that annoys us. Is anything wrong with that? Yes.

Take a moment and brainstorm: "What things do others do that bother me but that are not wrong or sinful and, thus, do not need to be forgiven?" Relationally healthy people can create a long list of answers to this question:

- chewing food too loudly
- forgetting someone's name
- vibrating your leg so that it shakes the next chair
- saying "I'm sorry" after every awkward moment
- having the sniffles and refusing to blow your nose
- not standing to one side if you're only riding an escalator (to let those who walk get by)
- putting the nearly empty milk carton back in the refrigerator
- wearing too much cologne or perfume

- neglecting to replace an empty toilet paper roll
- unnecessarily TYPING IN ALL CAPS (I'm testing you)
- standing too close in a checkout line
- incessantly clicking a pen
- heating fish in the microwave at work
- creating excessively long lists to prove a point
- starting group texts (okay, this one may require forgiveness)

The entire premise of this chapter is that we *forgive* sin, but we *excuse* mistakes and we *overlook* quirks. Oopsies don't need to be forgiven. We shouldn't cry (or yell) over spilled milk, nor is there any need to forgive the spiller of milk.

Using forgiveness to resolve relational irritants that are not moral in nature produces several bad results.

- Pride grows as we establish our preferences as the moral standard for others.
- Self-righteousness grows as we begin to feel like we have to forgive more often than we have to be forgiven.
- Judgmentalism grows as we gain an increasingly negative view of others.

To help us not overapply the practice of forgiveness, here are three sources of relational strain that do not call for a response of forgiveness.

1. HUMAN WEAKNESS

Being clumsy, succumbing to the degenerative influence of aging, being weak with a particular aptitude, experiencing the limitation of a physical illness or injury, immaturity in a child, and similar experiences are weaknesses. These things can be frustrating, but they're not sinful; therefore, they do not need to be forgiven.

The appropriate responses to human weakness are compassion, patience, and assistance. Friends should be able to discuss the impact that each other's weaknesses have on the other. Taking these conversations out of the moral sphere decreases the sense of shame commonly associated with our weaknesses. One of the most trust-building aspects of any relationship is the freedom to acknowledge our weakness and be loved anyway.

2. DIFFERENCES IN PERSONALITY OR PERSPECTIVE

Being extroverted vs. introverted, optimistic vs. pessimistic, risk averse vs. adventurous, concrete vs. abstract, or organized vs. fluid are all examples of differences in personality or perspective. These differences impact a relationship in many ways, but they are not moral, and, therefore, do not need to be forgiven.

The appropriate responses to differences in personality or perspective are appreciation, learning, and cooperation. Well managed and humbly discussed, these differences promote an iron-sharpening-iron dynamic within a relationship (Proverbs 27:17). Placing moral weight on personality differences idealizes one personality type. It is important to remember that Christlikeness can be exemplified through any personality type.[1]

3. ATTEMPTING TO DO SOMETHING AND FAILING

We may on occasion try to do something nice for a friend (i.e., cook a meal we haven't prepared before, help with home repair, etc.) and fail in the attempt to bless them. These moments may elicit a sense of disappointment, but they are not moral and, therefore, do not need to be forgiven.

The appropriate responses to these instances are affirmation and encouragement. Attempting to do a good thing and failing should still be viewed as a good thing. It is at least two steps ahead of attempting to do a bad thing and failing and one step ahead of being passive.

---

1. To read more about properly differentiating character qualities that exemplify Christlikeness and the qualities described by personality types, see "Is There a 'Jesus Personality'?" bradhambrick.com, July 1, 2014, http://bradhambrick.com/is-there-a-jesus-personality.

Responding to these unsuccessful attempts to do good is an essential part of creating an atmosphere in which both people feel free to take healthy relational risks. The freedom to fail is an important part of any healthy relationship. Overapplying forgiveness can throttle this freedom.

QUESTIONS FOR REFLECTION

1. Which negative effects of overapplying forgiveness (pride, self-righteousness, judgmentalism) are you most prone toward?
2. What is an example of when it would have been easy for you to moralize a moment of weakness, difference in personality, or unsuccessful attempt to do a good thing by offering forgiveness to resolve the tension of the moment?

Chapter 5

WHY WE SHOULDN'T FORGIVE MISINTERPRETATIONS

Read each of these statements and decide whether it is true or false:

- Forgiveness is always a virtue. True or false?
- Forgiveness can be destructive to a relationship. True or false?
- There are times when forgiving someone reinforces our pride or blindness. True or false?

(The correct answers are false, true, true.)

Can you think of examples when forgiveness is not a virtue, when forgiveness is harmful, or when forgiveness reinforces pride? Think through these scenarios.

- A husband feels hurt because his wife "disrespected" him when she asked a question about a decision. She genuinely didn't understand the decision because he did not adequately explain it.

- A wife feels hurt when her husband "failed to pursue" her when his plans for their anniversary did not measure up to her expectations (which she had never told him about).
- Friend A feels hurt when Friend B is "unwilling to invest in the relationship," but "investing" means matching the unhealthy, excessive commitment Friend A gives to the relationship.

In each of these brief vignettes, the person who is hurting might assume that, when they feel hurt, the Christian thing to do is to forgive, right? Can you tell that forgiveness might not be a God-honoring response? In each example, offering forgiveness would be harmful to both people in the relationship.

In each case the hurt being forgiven was based on a misinterpretation; forgiving would further ingrain this misinterpretation. Accepting the forgiveness offered would add a level of social reinforcement to the misinterpretation. So

1. if the husband says he forgives his wife, he would be under the continuing misconception that his communication about decisions was adequate and anything that aggravated his insecurities was disrespectful.
2. if the wife says she forgives her husband, she would continue to believe that a truly loving husband would intuitively know what his wife desires and that anything that disappointed her would be a sign that he wasn't pursuing her.
3. the friend would believe their excessive attention to their friend was the Christlike standard for selfless sacrifice and that everyone else should match their unsustainable level of involvement in the life of others.

The act of forgiving assumes the accuracy of one's assessment of the offense. Forgiveness is a morally laden action. It declares things not only bad (i.e., unpleasant or nonpreferential) but also wrong (i.e., against the character of God). If the moral assessment that undergirds the act of forgiving is inaccurate, then forgiving mischaracterizes God's assessment of the situation.

This may sound too strong, but let's think it through. Let's assume the husband/wife/friend in the examples above forgives the person who upset them. Let's also assume that the person they forgave verbalizes that they do not believe forgiveness is needed. Does the husband/wife/friend believe that God and the Bible is on their side of the disagreement? Yes, and now the husband/wife/friend has another reason to forgive (i.e., something to leverage against the other person)—resisting their initial willingness to forgive. God is further on their side.

WHAT IS THE DANGER?

You can begin to see the danger. Forgiving a misinterpretation reinforces the inaccurate perception. It even begins to align God with the misinterpretation. The misinterpretation becomes increasingly impenetrable (i.e., we're convinced we're right and are unwilling to see it any other way). If the other person won't agree with us, we view them as being hard-hearted and resistant to God's will.

Intentional or not, this is a form of manipulation. Even with the best of intentions, it contributes to the deterioration of the relationship.

WHAT IS MISSING?

These scenarios reveal a neglect of the guiding principles of Matthew 7:1–5, to take the log out of one's own eye first. When we fail to properly consider our role in a relational hardship, even our most biblical practices become destructive rather than helpful. Self-awareness is an essential component of applying the Scriptures to our life and relationships as God intended.

If we do not see ourselves or the situation accurately, we will not apply the Bible rightly to our life or our situation. We end up applying the Bible to a figment of our imagination. That is what is happening in each situation above. Forgiveness becomes a way that the husband/wife/friend tries to force the other person to live in their "alternate reality."

WHAT IS AN APPROPRIATE RESPONSE?

If you are on the receiving end of unhealthy forgiveness, a two-fold response is recommended: first, *empathy* toward the hurt and, second, an *invitation* to reconsider the interpretation.

An extension of forgiveness means the other person is hurt. Even if their interpretation is not true, their experience is real. A lack of empathy toward their hurt will only reinforce their interpretation that you are in the wrong.

We can only offer an invitation to reconsider the interpretation (i.e., reconsider any part we may have played in the misunderstanding). If we aggressively refute the interpretation, a conversation will become a debate. In the context of hurt, this has quite a low probability of being fruitful. Additionally, we offer this thoughtful reconsideration because our interpretation may be wrong. Hearing from the other person may reveal things we missed in our initial experience, and a response might sound like this: "I am very sorry that you are hurt. I'm not sure I understand yet why my response/action was wrong. I appreciate your desire to handle this situation with repentance and forgiveness. But can we walk back through what happened to assess what should have happened and what reasonable expectations/responses should have been?"

If the other person engages the conversation, there is an opportunity for both of you to learn and grow. Either or both of you may need to repent and forgive.

If you get a defensive or aggressive response and the situation warrants further discussion, you may need to say, "I don't think it's good for either of us if I accept your forgiveness without understanding how I was wrong. Would you be willing to meet with someone we both trust to help us figure this out?"

QUESTIONS FOR REFLECTION

1. How is it helpful to realize that the person who offers forgiveness is not always doing the most Christlike thing in that situation?

2. Can you remember an example where you were hurt and willing to forgive but later realized that what you perceived as hurtful was not morally wrong?

Section 2: Embracing God's Forgiveness

Have you ever tried to put together a puzzle without looking at the picture? Without a clear representation of the goal, it is quite difficult to put the pieces together. Trying to forgive others or embrace forgiveness from others without an accurate understanding of God's forgiveness is like missing the puzzle picture.

The goal of this section is to examine several common misunderstandings about God's forgiveness. This section may feel a bit like the ocean tide. Initially, you may be pulled in the direction of unrest as common concepts are deconstructed or put in a new light. Then, you may feel pulled toward comfort as you see the goodness of God's forgiveness in new ways.

Chapter 6

GOD'S FORGIVENESS TO US: UNCONDITIONAL?

"[F]orgive] one another, as God in Christ forgave you" (Ephesians 4:32). How we interpret this verse determines whether our conversations about forgiveness make wounds better or worse.

This verse means that everything we say about forgiveness is a direct reflection of the character of God. One way to rephrase this truth is that we are never more like Christ than when we forgive. But do we also understand the inverse implication of this truth; i.e., how we understand forgiveness is how we portray Christ? If our goal is to be more like Christ, this discussion has life-permeating implications. Let's look at several wrong ways this verse can be interpreted:

- Some people focus on the supreme act of love and use this verse to treat God like a grandfather writing a blank check. They tend to be "nice" people with enabling tendencies and have a hard time taking a stand on anything important—because, you know, love.

- Others focus on the severity of the sacrifice and strongly emphasize that we should do everything possible to avoid needing such a precious gift. It begins to feel shameful to need forgiveness. These tend to be legalists with strong convictions. They may be harsh, but they have the integrity to be just as hard on themselves as they are on everybody else.
- Some go so theologically "deep" with verses like this that everything becomes muddy. These are people who seem to believe God is most satisfied when the masses are most confused.
- Others stare at the verse in bewilderment. They don't know what it means, so they just do the best they can in any given situation and try not to blame God for much of anything that goes wrong.

Do any of these interpretations fit you? We all lean off-center in some direction. Self-awareness is an essential part of biblical application. If we don't see ourselves accurately, then we are likely to misapply the Bible.

Let's examine the question behind the bulleted examples above.

IS GOD'S FORGIVENESS UNCONDITIONAL?

Does the fact that there is no sin so bad that it is beyond God's ability to forgive mean that *unconditional* is the best adjective to describe God's forgiveness? No, this truth is about God's *capacity* to forgive. It is limitless. That is different from unconditional.

Does the reality that God delights in forgiving mean that his forgiveness is unconditional? No, this truth is about God's *willingness* to forgive. It brings him the most joy (Luke 15:7). That is different from being unconditional.

Do we get to set the terms of relationship with God? No; unless we repent (a condition), God does not forgive. God is not mocked (Galatians 6:7). We can't fake God out with tears or sorrowful language that is void of actual change (Matthew 3:7–10). If we try to convince God our sin is not wrong (changing the conditions), God doesn't budge. God admitted that the terms he sets are narrow (Matthew 7:14). Those who will not accept God's terms, even if they try to play nice with God, eventually run out of chances to accept his offer (Matthew 7:21–23).

God is infinitely generous in his forgiveness, but he is not unconditional. We have no reason to fear our sincere request for forgiveness will ever be denied. But we should not feel entitled to or cavalier about God's forgiveness.

GOD'S CONDITION OF FORGIVENESS IS LORDSHIP

God's forgiveness is not an "ollie, ollie oxen free" for everyone to go back to playing the game of life like they were before. *God's forgiveness is an invitation to a new way of life*. Those who reject this new way of life reject the terms of forgiveness.

Let's return to our simple definition of forgiveness—canceling a debt. God is not a banker who cancels a debt and says, "Keep running your business in the way that led to bankruptcy. Better luck next time." When God cancels the debt, he says, "Call me Lord. Follow the plan I have for life." If you are committed to a bankrupt lifestyle, the most loving thing God can do is limit how far into debt you go.

WHAT DOES THIS MEAN FOR US?

There are two implications for God's condition of forgiveness: one vertical and one horizontal.

First, vertically, *we have no reason to fear God withholding forgiveness*. No one who owns the wrongfulness of their sin, accepts Christ's payment for their sin, and embraces their need to follow Jesus as Lord will be denied. God understands his children follow him like clumsy toddlers. We fall often. But God absolutely delights when we follow him like children who imitate a loving father (Ephesians 5:1). Our soul can rest in this.

Second, horizontally, if God is not duped when he forgives, *we do not have to fear being forced into foolish forgiveness based on a theological technicality*. We do not have to fear a harmful person saying, "Because you're a Christian, you have to let me keep hurting you," and them being right.

In our efforts to forgive, we will not forgive perfectly; that is, "as God forgives us." There are several reasons for this:

- We do not know the heart of the person we're forgiving like God does.
- Our ability to remove hurt from the forefront of our mind is not perfect, like God's.
- Our desire to forgive is not as constant and benevolent as God's.
- Our ability to be hurt again may make the restoration process slower than it is for an omnipowerful God who has no relational needs.

These things may mean our forgiveness is a process, like every other part of our spiritual life. But too often, our fear of being hurt again because we unwisely forgive someone causes us to be suspicious of God's command. Much of this mistrust is rooted in misunderstanding God's forgiveness as being unconditional. We begin to think God is being weak and foolish and, therefore, is calling us to be weak and foolish like him. We see some of the things that God forgives (murder, adultery, betrayal, etc.) and think, surely, he got duped. We fear getting duped too.

God is not a fool, yet he does forgive. God does not ask us to be fools, but he does ask us to forgive. As we reflect further in this book, we will seek to further separate forgiveness from folly. The purpose of this chapter was simply to help you to see that God's call to forgive is not an expectation that you be relationally reckless.

QUESTIONS FOR REFLECTION

1. When have you seen the idea of God's forgiveness being unconditional misapplied? Was the other person not being precise with their words, or were they misrepresenting God's forgiveness?
2. What are the greatest points of comfort and reassurance that you took from this chapter?

Chapter 7

"FORGIVE AND FORGET" AND AN OMNISCIENT GOD

Memory after forgiveness is a dicey subject. We want to believe that God forgets our sin after we repent. We would like, after we forgive, to be able to forget sins other people commit against us. But we get angry and defensive when someone implies we should "be over it by now" or that remembering pain is inherently the same thing as bitterness. We're not sure how to unscramble this egg. Too often, conversations like this one get rushed. Being hurt and rushed at the same time is a combustible combination.

Let's return to our foundational premise: to forgive others as God in Christ forgave us (Ephesians 4:32). Does the Bible tell us anything about God's memory after he forgives? Hebrews 8:12 quotes Jeremiah 31:24 where God says, "I will be merciful toward their iniquities, and I will remember their sins no more." Is this an omniscient (i.e., all-knowing) God promising to forget?

At one level, God couldn't have erased his memories of Israel's sin, or he wouldn't remember the iniquities toward which he had been merciful. It doesn't make sense that a God who knows every event of our lives (Psalm 139) could forget our sin. In 2 Corinthians

5:10 we learn that, when we get to heaven, we will stand before Jesus and give an account for how we lived, both the good and bad parts of our lives.

So what is God promising? He is promising to be merciful and that after forgiveness, when God sees us, he does not view us through the identity of "sinner" but through the identity of an "adopted child." God promises that when he sees us he will "not remember" our sin—not have our sin at the front of his mind.

The promise of forgiveness means that a Christian never has to worry about what is on God's mind when he looks at us. Our eyes can gaze into God's eyes when we pray without any sense of shame or condemnation.

That is the kind of forgiveness we are called to strive toward. Like every other part of our Christian maturation (sanctification), it is a process. But when it comes to our memory, how do we make progress toward forgiving like Christ forgave us?

GOD DOESN'T "CHANGE TEAMS"

We start by realizing that God doesn't change teams when we need to forgive. It is easy to feel like God is on "our team" when we are hurt; that is, we feel God's compassion toward us. But we often feel like God changes teams as soon as the shock of the offense is over and forgiveness becomes a possibility. It's like God moves from being compassionate to being demanding. This, of course, is not true.

WHAT IS THE GOAL OF FORGIVENESS?

Next, we realize that our goal is different from what we think. We think we have to forget, but our goal is simply to resist defining the offender by what they did when we see them or think about them. If we see friend, sibling, parent, or coworker instead of liar, cheater, coward, or drunk and can be merciful toward them, we are forgiving like Christ forgave us.

So your first concern is not how to forgive but rather to recognize who the person is and what role they play in your life. Later, we will grapple with the restoration of trust. At this stage, we're not implying that forgiveness means total trust—forgive and forget. We're simply saying there is more to this person than the pain they caused, and it's healthy for us to remember that.

PACE FORGIVENESS

In the process of forgiveness, how do we begin interacting in a cordial, civil way with the person we're striving to forgive? The answer to this question is a first step. We shouldn't get so intimidated by the fifth, seventh, or thirteenth step in the process that we fail to take the first. We'll learn some things when taking the first step that will determine the direction of the second and third steps. When Jesus talks about loving our enemies, he starts with the action step of simply greeting them (Matthew 5:47).

In the process of forgiving, it's okay only to be cordial for a while. See the person for who they are, rather than for what they did. A truly repentant person won't rush you and should respond to grace with appreciation. Allow God to generate warmth in you from the appreciation in them. Also, remember that their repentance is a process, just like your forgiveness. This means that progress in one person should encourage progress in the other.

Hopefully, you can see this idea of pacing as a good thing—good for you and good for the person you are forgiving. If your friend is having a hard time getting this choreographed dance of forgiveness and repentance, invite them to read this chapter. If they say it's dumb and rush you and feel entitled to your trust, then you have a glimpse that their repentance may not be wholehearted. But if they see how progressive restoration mirrors progressive forgiveness, it will improve communication and adjust expectations for both of you moving forward.

FORGETTING

How close can we get to forgetting sins against us? The answer will vary from person to person and offense to offense, but a background dynamic to what we've been discussing merits our attention.

The more we repeat something in our minds, the more ingrained the memory becomes. This means that one way (not the only way) to identify bitterness is the degree of detail we remember about the offense over time. Greater memory requires frequent rehearsing.

The discussion above touched on four points:

1. See the person as a person, not as their offense.
2. In mercy, relate to them cordially based on their role in your life.
3. Allow their response of appreciation to develop warmth toward them.
4. Let this process facilitate healthy restoration over time.

Do you see what is absent from this strategy? Rehearsing the offense. Fixating on what you need to forgive makes it harder to forgive.

"Is this safe? Can this process help me move forward without undue risk of getting hurt again?" you (wisely) ask. If the other person is not repentant, that shows up at point 3. You refrain from moving forward based on their lack of healthy repentance. You can respond wisely and still maintain the emotional benefits of points 1 and 2.

Jesus did this frequently. He invited people into relationship but did not accept disingenuous or manipulative engagement (Luke 6:46–49). Jesus was willing, even eager, to forgive. That's why he came to earth (Philippians 2:1–11). But if someone's actions revealed a duplicitous heart, he "did not entrust himself to them" (John 2:24). Sometimes Jesus even did this with people he was fond of (Mark 10:20–22).

This means you can trust forgiveness. When we've been hurt, sometimes we mistrust the idea of forgiveness as much as we mistrust the person who hurt us. One of my goals in this book is to help restore your trust toward forgiveness so that you can know the freedom and healing God wants to give you through forgiving.

QUESTIONS FOR REFLECTION

1. Does God really forgive and forget? What does he expect you to do with the painful memories of the things you forgive?
2. How is mistrusting the idea of forgiveness different from mistrusting the person?

Chapter 8

INTRAPERSONAL FORGIVENESS: SHOULD I FORGIVE MYSELF?

Let's start by asking, "Can we be in debt to ourselves?" If our primary metaphor for forgiveness is canceling a debt, it makes sense to ask, "Can someone be both the debtor and the lender in the same transaction?"

At one level, it doesn't matter if we can be both the debtor and the lender in the same transaction. Regardless, guilt and shame can still plague us even after we've done business with God and every other relevant person. This experience can be emotionally and relationally debilitating. Whatever that experience is, we need to know how to deal with it.

That is the relevance of the first question above. We are unlikely to solve a problem we miscategorize. If we view ourselves as being in debt to ourselves and that is not the case, we are unlikely to make progress. Many people approach questions about self-forgiveness as if it were a theological riddle to solve. The conversation gets convoluted; we hope confusion will distract us from our guilt. Categorization is not about passing a theology quiz; it is about identifying the best-fit remedy God has to offer.

So what kind of problem are we facing when we say, "I just can't forgive myself"? There is not one answer because this phrase does not capture only one experience. We will consider five possible emotional obstacles captured in the idea of self-forgiveness.

1. AMBIGUOUS REPENTANCE

Sometimes we mistake *emotions* of deep sorrow for the *conversation* of repentance. Repentance is not a feeling. It is a conversation. If we address our sorrow to "whom it may concern" (meaning no one), we should not expect any emotional resolution.

Ambiguous repentance expects to get emotional relief from feeling bad enough for long enough. That is like expecting to get to the top of a hill by being still enough for long enough. Have you had a conversation of repentance with God and those harmed by your sin?

2. PENANCE

Penance is more active than ambiguous repentance. Actually, it is much more active. This obstacle gets caught in the trap of measurement. We know what we did was "real bad," and we try to do a lot to make it better. But we're never quite sure when "a lot" is "enough," so we feel compelled to do more or feel worse to prove we're not minimizing our sin.

The remedy here is to realize *Jesus did enough because we never could*. Our response is accepting Christ's gift with humility. A derivative problem emerges here. We tend to think of humility as anti-pride—a greasy, self-deprecating disposition. If that is the essence of humility, then humility would be a form of emotional self-abuse as we berate ourselves. We need a positive definition of humility, not just its antonym. Humility is an enjoyable combination of an accurate view of self (strengths and weaknesses, successes and failures), concern for others (non–self-centered), and openness to new ideas (ability to engage life with curiosity).[1] Ironically, as you

1. For more on a positive definition of humility, see Mark R. McMinn, *The Science of Virtue: Why Positive Psychology Matters to the Church* (Grand Rapids, MI: Brazos Press, 2017), chap. 4.

read this definition, you realize that humility doesn't draw attention to itself. It is free to enjoy life and other people.

3. MISTAKING CONSEQUENCES FOR PUNISHMENT

There are also times when the dominoes from our sin continue to fall (i.e., committing adultery, which destroys your family and harms your children, or conducting yourself at work in a way that results in getting fired and facing the challenges of a lost income). We feel like we "can't catch a break." Ongoing consequences leave us in a chronic state of regret. Regret feels so much like guilt that we begin to think the remedy is to forgive ourselves.

In this case, grief is the more appropriate response. We need to grieve the loss of a future that would have been if we had not committed the sin. Sometimes we feel awkward grieving the consequences of sin as if that means we weren't really sorry. We're not talking about grieving the absence of sin; that is a contradiction to repentance. We're talking about grieving the ongoing mess sin makes.

Grieving the consequences of sin is much like any other grief. It concludes with a sense of resolution and an embrace of the life ahead despite the loss. Allow yourself to embrace God's compassion toward you regarding these consequences. Consequences are not a sign of God's continuing anger. That was settled when you embraced God's forgiveness. For regret, healthy grief can do what self-forgiveness never will.

4. PRIDE

We must admit, at times we hold our own opinion above all others. This is what happens when we say, "I know God has forgiven me, but I just can't forgive myself." We are holding our opinion above the ultimate opinion. We are not allowing God to have the last word on our moral failures.

The remedy for this form of pride is the same as for all other forms of pride: submitting to the lordship of Christ. It means we take God's pronouncement of forgiveness of our sin as the final word on the matter. If you will, God is the Supreme Court for our sin. Once the high court rules on the matter, the rulings of lower courts are rendered moot.

5. CONTINUING TO SIN

Finally, we can say we are having trouble forgiving ourselves as a coded way of admitting we're still committing the sin. We are plagued by guilt because we are still guilty. In this case, our conscience is acting just like it should. Saying we need to forgive ourselves is to misjudge our conscience as being in error when it's our actions that are wrong.

The solution here is disclosure and repentance, not self-forgiveness. Our conscience is alerting us to two sins: the sin for which we feel guilty and the sin of hiding that sin. It is the second sin that is the greater problem. While honesty may be frightening, it is also liberating.

FINAL QUESTION

Now, you may say, "I've wrestled with these things. I believe I have honored the solutions to each of the things listed. But I am still not experiencing emotional freedom." That may be true. Emotions can become as habituated as behaviors. Guilt (or any other emotion) can become as instinctual as chewing our fingernails.

So I invite you to ask more questions: "How would I live if I were forgiven? What would I be doing differently?" Make a list of the answers. Perhaps it's "engage my hobbies more" or "look friends in the eye" or "ask more authentic questions with friends." Put as many things on the list as you can. Intentionally do those things. Then allow your emotions to follow your actions.

As Christians, we often want change to move from heart to mind to hand; that is, from values to beliefs to actions. This is one path of change, but it is not the only path of change. Change can also move from hand to mind to heart—that is, from actions to healthier emotions to a healthier identity. It may be your path to relief is to do the things a forgiven person does (actions) while reminding yourself these actions are appropriate (beliefs) until you feel the peace of being forgiven (emotions). If you looked at the five areas listed here and did not get relief, then this second path is likely your journey.

QUESTIONS FOR REFLECTION

1. Of the five experiences often mistaken for self-forgiveness, to which are you most prone?
2. Can you think of a time when change moved from hand to mind to heart instead of heart to mind to hand?

Section 3: Wisely Extending Forgiveness

We have spent two sections of this book defining the concept of forgiveness and reflecting on the implications of God's forgiveness of us. We've mentioned forgiving others from time to time but mostly by way of foreshadowing or drawing implications. This is where we turn the corner and focus on the gritty work of forgiving others. While definitions of forgiveness are clear, and God's forgiveness is reliable and consistent, when another person gets involved forgiveness begins to feel risky, unpredictable.

In this section, we apply wisdom to forgiving others. Wisdom cannot guarantee an outcome, but it can mitigate risk. Like the biblical command to be generous, we want to obey the command to forgive wisely. Being generous to the point of bankruptcy is not virtuous, but that is not a license to be stingy. Similarly, forgiving to the point of being a doormat is not virtuous, but that is not a license to disregard forgiveness. We need wisdom, so we'll engage hard questions about hard situations.

Chapter 9

THE UNCOMFORTABLE REALITY: FORGIVENESS IS NEVER DESERVED

We must grapple with the uncomfortable reality that no one deserves forgiveness, and we may never think it's "a good time" to forgive. I don't think I've ever heard someone say, "You know, I realized I haven't been offended in a long time. I was praying that God would give me the opportunity to forgive again soon, so I wouldn't get rusty at it. Thank you for [some expression of interpersonal offense]." If you think that way, you're further down the sanctification highway than most of us.

On top of that, the last significant thing the offender did toward you was wrong enough that Jesus had to die for it. Remember, we don't forgive mistakes; we forgive sin. This person is not on a good streak in our life. That's three strikes: (1) They don't deserve forgiveness, (2) this isn't a good time, and (3) the last thing they did was rotten. I'm two paragraphs into this chapter, and we're both in a bad mood.

That's good, though, because that's where forgiveness occurs, in a moody-angry-withdrawn-sulky funk. We all have our preferred flavor of funk, but funky is going to be our emotional climate when we need to forgive.

Believe it or not, this is a helpful realization. Sometimes we fall into the trap of thinking that doing the right thing will inherently feel good. While plausible, we quickly realize many of the most important right things we do don't feel good. Telling the truth is often uncomfortable. Saving money is rarely pleasurable. Don't even get me started on exercise. The emotional confirmation of having done the right thing often comes later.

When we realize this, we have removed one of the emotional obstacles to forgiveness. That doesn't make the journey easy. But every five-pound weight we can remove from the hundred-pound load we're carrying makes the journey easier. Thank you for persevering.

FROM HEAVY TO HEALTHY

This image of carrying a load helps us frame an important question: How much of the hundred-pound load should come off when I get up the nerve to say the three little words, "I forgive you"? The answer will vary from person to person and situation to situation. Forgiving a boss in a bad work environment you can't change is likely to create less relief than forgiving a friend who is remorseful for what they did.

Our motive for forgiving—that Christ has forgiven us—helps here. We forgive primarily (sometimes exclusively) to honor Christ. The other person is merely the recipient of our obedience to God. We can delight in what we're giving even if we are less than enthused about who we're giving it to. It's not ideal, but it may be where we are right now. That's a five-pound weight off our load.

What is another five-pound weight that comes off when we forgive? Deliberation. When we make the decision to forgive, we can quit debating with ourselves. It often takes more cognitive air-time and emotional energy to not forgive than it does to forgive.

In that sense, forgiving is good emotional hygiene. Even secular mental health professionals advocate for the positive effects of forgiveness: healthier relationships, improved mental health, less anxiety, lower blood pressure, fewer symptoms of depression, a stronger immune system, and improved heart health.[1] Forgiveness may be as health-promoting as jogging for thirty minutes three times a week, and is much less sweaty.

So let's boil it down to a tip-the-scale question if we're still struggling to forgive. Can we want good for the person who offended us? Desiring good for the other person is the root of empathy, which is the seed of forgiveness. We have been unloading our pack to be able to make this jump.

Unforgiveness says some combination of, "I want bad for you. I would be disappointed if good things happened to you. I want you to suffer in ways that are comparable to how you made me feel. You are a distraction from me enjoying a normal day. The world would feel morally out of order if good things happen to you."

Forgiveness says some combination of, "I want good for you. I want you to come to know God's forgiveness and freedom. I want God to change you into the kind of person who would not do again what you did, and then I want you to flourish. I want the freedom to enjoy the good things in my life without comparing them to the good things in your life."

If you have this level of empathy for the person who hurt you, then you are ready to forgive. In that sense, forgiveness is getting out from in between the person who hurt you and God. Your forgiveness doesn't predispose God to be more gracious to them anymore than your unforgiveness prompts God to be less gracious toward them.

1. "Forgiveness: Letting Go of Grudges and Bitterness," mayoclinic. org, November 13, 2020, https://www.mayoclinic.org/healthy-lifestyle/ adult-health/in-depth/forgiveness/art-20047692.

You may be asking questions about trust and how much to restore the relationship. Those are important questions and topics we will pick up in the next few chapters. But for now, consider taking some of the load off your pack by forgiving.

QUESTIONS FOR REFLECTION

1. How does it help you realize that when you need to forgive you may not be in a good place emotionally? What pressure does it alleviate? What excuses does it remove?

2. Does reframing forgiveness in the simple statement, "I want good, not ill, for the person who hurt me," make forgiveness seem more doable? How much cognitive or emotional freedom would embracing that statement provide for you?

Chapter 10

CAN BOUNDARIES AND FORGIVENESS COEXIST?

Christians have often struggled with how to think about boundaries in broken relationships. Some use the word *boundaries* to communicate that Christians don't have to be doormats just because we want to model grace. Others resist the concept of boundaries to emphasize that Jesus crossed all barriers to rescue us in our rebelliousness; likewise, Christians are called to model this same love to the lost world.

Both perspectives make valid points. As we think about wisely applying the implications of forgiveness, we need to discern how to honor what is right in both approaches. Let's consider four principles that can help us think wisely about boundaries and forgiveness.

1. BOUNDARIES SEPARATE WISDOM FROM FOLLY

Boundaries, by definition, divide things. The question is what is being divided? If we think of boundaries as dividing people, it is hard to reconcile the two approaches above. But a healthy concept of boundaries views the barrier being placed between wisdom and folly rather than between you and me.

After forgiveness, the hesitancy in restoring trust is not whether I'm willing to have anything to do with you but, rather, whether you will honor the principles of healthy relationship. When an addict insists on carrying cash or a controlling person refuses to seek outside advice, they are violating how wisdom would curb their destructive patterns.

I am not rejecting you or giving up on you if I refuse to enable foolishness. However, if you insist on living foolishly, you will find yourself on the other side of my boundary from folly. In this sense, a synonym for *boundaries* would be "reasonable expectations" or "limits of wisdom."

Read Proverbs. A chapter a day will get you through the whole book in a month. As you read, underline every use of the word *fool*, *foolishness*, and *folly* (or comparable language). Pay attention to the instructions that accompany the fool-family of words. They are cautionary. One means of God's protection for you is his warning against folly. We appreciate the protection but at the same time are grieved when adhering to the warnings creates distance between us and those we love.

2. BOUNDARIES ARE AN INVITATION

Boundaries, when rightly communicated, are an invitation, not a rejection. You are inviting the other person to cross over the line from folly to wisdom. Thinking of boundaries this way will help you communicate your limits in a more receivable manner.

When you are confident in what you will and will not do, pressure from others becomes less threatening. You can begin to say, "I will not [describe the unhealthy expectation; for instance, have an argument via text message], but I will be happy to [describe a healthy alternative; for instance, meet you at a restaurant to discuss our differences]." In this sense you are not "enforcing" the boundary (as if you were the boundary police); you are providing another opportunity for the other person to choose wisdom over folly.

This is where we often get hung up. We think this approach makes our forgiveness conditional. It doesn't; it makes trust conditional. Forgiveness does not commit me to an unwise or destructive pattern of relating. If someone will not receive your invitation to healthy relationship, they are rejecting biblical wisdom; you are not rejecting them. Their refusal to move from folly to wisdom is what creates the distance.

3. BOUNDARIES AS EMOTIONAL WALLS ARE UNHEALTHY

The word *boundaries* can have many different meanings. Sometimes the word is used to refer to emotional walls we put up against anyone getting close or really knowing us, in order to protect ourselves from hurt.

This use of the term *boundaries*, while understandable after being hurt, prevents us from experiencing the kind of healthy relationships God intends to be restorative. Boundaries, in this sense, do not protect us from folly but insulate us from authentic relationships.

From this principle we learn something about recovering from destructive relationships. The coping mechanisms that protect us in dysfunctional relationships are often disruptive to healthy relationships. Ask yourself, "What did I learn I must do to 'keep the peace' in the destructive relationship?" You might answer never share my opinion to prevent anger, avoid new people to prevent jealousy, or don't try new things to prevent being shamed if you fail.

Now ask yourself, "What impact does withholding my opinion, avoiding new people, or abstaining from new activities have on the possibility and quality of healthy relationships?" The rules we learn to play by in unhealthy relationships can prevent the establishment of healthy relationships. This use of the term *boundaries* is one that we need to learn to resist.

4. BOUNDARIES AREN'T FOR EVERYTHING

The benefits associated with setting boundaries do not mean that boundaries are a universal tool for relationships. To use the idea of boundaries well, we need the ability to distinguish felt needs from real needs. Real needs are the things required to make life safe or sustainable. Felt needs are the things that make an adequate life better. Real needs are essential. Felt needs are good.

Boundaries are for unsafe contexts. If we apply the concept of boundaries to felt needs, we begin to treat everything that hurts our feelings as unsafe. Sometimes people disappoint us. That's sad but not dangerous. We don't need to create a boundary for that. If we treat as dangerous everything we don't like, people will begin to treat us like the relational "boy or girl who cried wolf."

This doesn't mean that felt needs are unimportant. Healthy relationships seek to honor felt needs. But the means for doing so is awareness-building, compromise, and balanced give-and-take for each other's preferences, rather than establishing boundaries.

It also means that when boundaries are needed because someone is refusing to move from folly to wisdom, we should not expect that person to meet our felt needs. They are not displaying the maturity to be relied upon in this way. Instead, we grieve the condition of this relationship and find other ways to fulfill these legitimate desires.

QUESTIONS FOR REFLECTION

1. Which of the four principles of boundaries capture the way you most naturally think of the concept or most frequently hear other people use it? How do all four principles together help balance the concept?
2. Think of several relationally challenging situations you've experienced that remained strained after forgiveness. What would a balanced application of these four principles look like in those situations?

Chapter 11

FORGIVENESS AND MANIPULATIVE REPENTANCE

We have been reflecting on the restoration of trust after forgiveness. We are skittish about restoring trust because we have all, to some extent, been burned by manipulative repentance—that is, when the person who hurt us says they're sorry, but they really just want the relationship to return to its unhealthy patterns. It is often hard to put into words what was unhealthy in these interactions, which only adds to our hesitancy. Our goal in this chapter is to identify key markers of manipulative repentance.

To acknowledge healthy and unhealthy forms of repentance is both common sense and biblical (2 Corinthians 7:8–13). On this, everyone—secular and sacred—agrees. The difficulty is in discerning disingenuous repentance. Mature and discerning people can witness the same conversation and walk away with distinctly different impressions about whether a given expression of remorse represents genuine repentance, sorrow for being caught, or a tactic to gain relational leverage.

A number of phrases can point to manipulative repentance. Before looking at them, let's consider two common misconceptions that tend to blind us to manipulative repentance:

The first misconception is that manipulation is about method. This misconception can be corrected by understanding that manipulation is about *why* or how something is done (motive) more than *what* is said or done (method). There is no exhaustive list of manipulative phrases. Every phrase listed below has a context in which it could be legitimate and appropriate. The goal of manipulation lies in the motive (e.g., to resist change, to minimize responsibility, to blame shift) and is effective at fooling the person being manipulated because the phrases can be used innocently.

The second misconception is that manipulation requires forethought. Manipulation does not require careful planning or intellectual cunning. Many people who are using remorse to gain an advantage or avoid responsibility are not aware of what they're doing. Their immediate goal is to escape the discomfort of the moment. This desire to escape shapes the way they define words and frame questions. That is what manipulation is: defining words and framing questions (by verbiage or emotions) in such a way that makes a healthy response from the other person seem selfish, mean, or unreasonable.

MANIPULATIVE REPENTANCE?

Seven statements follow that may point to manipulative repentance.

1. "I know I'm not perfect."

This phrase communicates, "Your expectations that I respond decently (e.g., speak kindly, fulfill my commitments, be honest about my schedule, etc.) are unreasonable. You are holding me to a perfectionistic standard. To avoid being confronted by you, I would have to be perfect. You should feel bad for being judgmental and harsh."

The phrase "I know I'm not perfect" frames an expectation that the other person owns their faults as an expectation that they never sin. Offering forgiveness does not require that someone never sin. It does require that they be humble about their sin and committed to growing.

2. "I've never pretended to be someone I'm not."

This phrase communicates, "You knew who I was when we started this relationship, so you are being unfair by expecting me to be decent."

This confuses genuineness with righteousness, authenticity with holiness. By this standard, someone could be consistently hurtful, and we would still be to blame for their sin because we chose to be in relationship with them. But we would also be condemned as "unforgiving" for ending the relationship. The question is not whether I know your persistent patterns of behavior but whether those patterns honor God and others.

3. "You are bringing up stuff from the past."

This phrase communicates, "We can only talk about events, not patterns of behaviors."

Often this impasse is reached when the individual going through the motions of repentance is unwilling to see that the offense (e.g., intoxication or belligerence) was part of a larger pattern (e.g., addiction or abusive speech). If there is a pattern of behavior and this pattern goes unacknowledged, then the other person is, in effect, demanding that we respond to every instance as the first occurrence.

4. "You know I am not the kind of person who would do that . . . that is not what I meant."

This phrase communicates, "Your experience of me is not an accurate depiction of reality. My self-perception and intentions are more accurate than your experience."

These phrases leave the supposedly repenting person in charge of defining the event for which forgiveness is being sought. For instance, if we're addressing stalking behavior, the manipulatively repentant person might say, "You know I wouldn't do that. I was just trying to make sure you were safe. I was worried about you. I'm sorry if it made you uncomfortable." The self-perception of the sinner (i.e., making sure you're safe) is being imposed as a limit on how their actions are interpreted (i.e., can't be stalking). The result is that the offended person loses voice in describing their pain. The offending person remains in charge of the narrative.

5. "I said I was sorry. What more do you want from me?"

This phrase communicates, "If anything more than my words (e.g., 'I'm sorry') is required in response to my actions, then you are unforgiving, mean, weak, or hyperemotional."

This phrase often implies that an apology should be met with an immediate sense of trust and equanimity in the relationship. Any lingering sense of mistrust by the offended person is then labeled as an unreasonable and ungodly form of punishment.

You will also notice more use of first-person pronouns (e.g., I, me, my) than second-person pronouns (e.g., you, your). An excessive use of self-referential pronouns may reveal that the person repenting is focusing on their personal experience of the offense more than on the impact on the person they hurt or offended.

Notice, first person pronouns should be used in the active/ownership part of repentance.[1] However, in the description of the impact and aftermath of our sin, healthy repentance focuses more on the disruption we caused in the other person's life. For instance, healthy repentance sounds like, "I [first person pronoun] realize when I [describe sin accurately and nondefensively] it was wrong [ownership] and hurt you by [describing effects]."

6. "There are a lot of people/couples who have it much worse than you/we do."

This phrase communicates, "You should feel bad for complaining when the situation was not as bad as it could have been."

---

1. This chapter is about navigating manipulative repentance as an obstacle to healthy forgiveness. If you want corresponding material on genuine and robust repentance, see "7 Marks of a Good Apology vs. 8 Marks of a Bad Apology," bradhambrick.com, May 15, 2018, http://bradhambrick.com/7-marks-of-a-good-apology-vs-8-marks-of-a-bad-apology/.

This equates "could have been worse" with "not bad enough to mention." It also portrays suffering as a competitive sport in which only those who suffer the worst merit sympathy for their hardship.

This phrase often comes toward the end of a manipulative repentance conversation. Early in the conversation, the repenting person minimizes or blame-shifts. When the offended party tries to clarify the degree of hurt, this is viewed as exaggeration. This perception of exaggeration leads the repenting person to use the logic that "this situation is not as bad as [something they consider to be worse]."

7. "I promise I will do better (without agreement on the problem or concrete examples)."

This phrase communicates, "Even though I minimize and disagree with you about the past and present, you should trust what I mean when I say 'better' about the future."

Commitments to change are not bad, although these commitments should have more humility than an absolute promise. It is better and more accurate to say, "I will work on not [offensive behavior] by [specific actions toward change and accountability from mutually trusted people]," than "I will never do that again." However, if generic commitments to do "better" are made during a disagreement, these commitments become a way to shut down communication. If someone says with exasperation, "Fine! I'll do better next time. Can we just drop it?" they are not repenting. They are ending the conversation.

CONCLUSION

The question remains how do we respond to manipulative repentance? If the relationship is safe, then we can use the concepts above to describe the unhealthy dynamic in their words and respond according to their response.

If the offending person acknowledges the coerciveness in their words, we can ask them to try again without blame-shifting or minimizing.

If the offending person will not acknowledge the coerciveness of words, then we should respond to them in whatever manner would be wisest toward an unrepentant person who was sinning in that way. Until they can express ownership for their initial offense and contrition without manipulation, they are not repentant.

QUESTIONS FOR REFLECTION

1. Which of the two misconceptions are you most prone to believe?
2. Which of the seven phrases are you most prone to use? How would you respond if someone used them when repenting to you?

Chapter 12

TRUST AS A PROPORTIONAL VIRTUE

In this chapter, we are going to grapple with the restoration of trust after forgiveness. We will be assessing a common misunderstanding of trust that can cause us to inadvertently rush the person who has been hurt. When we talk about trust as a virtue in this chapter, we are grappling with the sense of guilt we sometimes experience when we say, "I feel bad for not trusting [person] after [offense]," when we want to trust more than we intuitively know we should.

Simply put, trust is a *proportional* virtue. The alternative to a proportional virtue is an *absolute* virtue. For example, honesty is an absolute virtue. You should always be honest (sometimes with more tact than others, if for instance, you are evaluating your children's artwork). There is never a time when we would say it is good to lie.[1]

---

1. Extreme situations exist when dishonesty protects something of greater value. For instance, in The Hiding Place, the Ten Boom family lied to Nazi soldiers about hiding Jews, who would have been taken to concentration camps during the Holocaust. In a broken world, even absolute virtues, such as honesty and protecting life, can be in tension with one another. But most of our struggles to trust are not at this extreme.

That gives us a contrast for understanding what it means for trust to be a proportional virtue. It is good (i.e., wise) to trust someone in proportion to their trustworthiness. It is foolish or naive to trust someone *more than* they are trustworthy. It does not represent Christ well to that person and gives them a falsely positive assessment of their life choices. When we treat the virtue of trust (proportional) like the virtue of honesty (absolute), we rush restoration.

Let's seek to understand the idea of proportional trust a bit more before we consider the relational implications. We will begin with a numeric scale, which is more concrete than life ever can be. Let's assume you have a friend who is 70 percent trustworthy. Wise trust relates to them with 65–75 percent trust; 50 percent trust is too skeptical, and 90 percent trust is naive.

The illustration is clear but not practical. Our friends don't come with trustworthiness meters above their heads like characters in a video game. However, if we understand the point better, that's progress. We can now see that overtrusting and undertrusting can be equally problematic. In a discussion about forgiveness, we can be prone to only see the problem with undertrusting.

Imagine you have an adult child who struggles with alcohol addiction. They are willing to admit it's a problem and attend a support group. But they resist being transparent about their schedule, insist on carrying cash, and keep in touch with several close drinking buddies.

For the purposes of this discussion, we'll say you forgave them for years of lying about their addictive habits and the defaming things they said about you while creating a drunken scene at the recent family reunion. But, how much do you trust them? Now the concept of proportional trust allows us to ask better questions. Trust is no longer all-or-nothing. What responses of trust would affirm the good steps they are willing to take? What responses of trust would falsely affirm that their current efforts are adequate?

This example is too truncated to go into much detail. Based on the information given, however, it would be too soon to force the adult child to move out of the house but naive to allow them to borrow money. The parents should be willing to *both* affirm their child for their good choices *and* willing to address the wise choices the adult child is still unwilling to make.

You can tell, as if you didn't already know it, how messy trust can be. The point is not that every family would (or even should) make the exact same decision in this situation. The point is that parents should, even after forgiving, think principally and proportionally about what wise trust looks like in response to their adult child's some-good-some-bad responses to a drinking problem.

Now, let's return to the idea that all-or-nothing trust is unwise for the parents and unhealthy for the adult child (sticking with the example above). If trust were an absolute virtue, the parents would *either* say they forgive their child for the family reunion fiasco and treat them like everything was fine *or* say they refuse to forgive because they cannot trust their child's incomplete approach to addressing the problem.

You can quickly see that if we treat forgiveness as tightly correlated with trust and trust as an absolute virtue, things do not go well for the person on either side of the relational strain. The parents would either be harsh or permissive. Neither is optimal for their child. We can see this in an anonymous case study, but how often do we get trapped in an either-or mindset when forgiveness gets personal?

So, what does a conversation sound like when the child, in this example, asks the parents to borrow money? It might sound something like this:

> "We're proud of you for being willing to admit you've had a problem with drinking. That takes courage and humility. We appreciate how you've been engaging in recovery. We want to encourage you to continue with that. That's why we're happy to have you at home and provide room

and board. If you stay engaged with recovery, you don't have to worry about that changing.

"But you have chosen not to be open about your schedule, insisted on carrying cash so we don't know how you spend your money, and hang out with friends who have encouraged your drinking. Giving you additional money would be more trust than the quality of your current choices warrants. We want to trust you more, but we believe it is best for everyone if our trust is proportional to your commitment to change. We love you, and that's why we're not going to loan you money."

This example goes into details (like any form of trust always does), but notice the pattern:

- affirm good/wise choices
- articulate your corresponding actions of trust
- identify the problematic behaviors/choices
- explain why proportional trust is the loving response

Though the details may change from situation to situation, the outline is transferable to most situations.

After a proportional assessment, having a plan for a principle-based response helps us be calm, warm, and compassionate in how we communicate. We do not want our response (too cold or too hot) to become a distraction from the wisdom we are trying to apply. When we bring a better disposition to the conversation, it gives a difficult conversation a much better opportunity to be effective.

A brief discussion like this cannot create the script of what you need to say. It can, however, allow you to reconcile one of the factors that frequently causes you to feel like "tough love" is unloving.

QUESTIONS FOR REFLECTION

1. How would you explain to a friend the idea of trust being a proportional virtue?
2. Can you think of a few examples of when this concept would have helped someone emotionally reconcile with a wiser approach to a difficult situation?

Chapter 13

IDENTIFYING WISE TRUST ON A SPECTRUM

Metaphorically speaking, there are "degrees" on the thermometer of trust—stages in trust recovery. In this chapter, we will offer a proposal for what those stages might be. The progression this chapter offers begins with a relationship at its most trust-broken point.

Not all violations of trust should require starting at this lowest point. As you read through this progression, there are two key questions to ask: (1) When things were at their worst, what stage of wise trust was warranted? and (2) What does wise trust look like now? The progress you have already made should be a source of encouragement for the journey ahead; both hope that you won't be rushed and that progress is possible.

Movement through this progression can be compared to a dance between the other person's efforts at change and your willingness to take relational risks. Change in either person alone will not create trust. Neither growth in the other person alone nor your own willingness to take a relational risk alone will create trust. The dance may not be one step by the other person followed by one step by you. But unless both of you are moving, the two of you are not dancing.

STAGES OF TRUST RECOVERY

Stage 1: Third-Party Mediation

At this level of trust brokenness, you do not feel safe, at least emotionally, to be with the other person without someone else present. At this stage, trust is built as you hear the other person being honest about their sin with someone you trust (perhaps a counselor, pastor, or mutually trusted friend) and being willing to receive correction or instruction from that person. Having the third party there gives you the sense of security to be honest about your perspective. As the person who hurt you cooperates, you begin to trust them vicariously through the trust that you have for the third party.

Stage 2: Listen and Validate

Now you are willing to have a one-on-one conversation with the person who hurt you, but you are skeptical of most everything they say. You don't believe them; you believe facts. If they have facts to back up what they say, you will trust that much and little more. This is a tedious way to communicate, but the inconvenience feels necessary to avoid pain. Any statement that is not factual (e.g., a future promise, an interpretation of an event, an expression of feeling) is viewed as deceptive, manipulative, or insulting. As a pattern of validated facts emerge, you begin to trust that there is a commitment to honesty and transparency.

Stage 3: Listen and Require Less Validation

Listening to the person who hurt you now feels like less work. The rate at which you are searching for questions and processing information is decreasing. Giving the benefit of the doubt for things you are uncertain about may still feel unnatural and dangerous. Any statement that is incomplete or slanted too positively is often assumed to be intentional deceit and creates a trust regression. As the other person's statements prove to be accurate, the practical necessities of life create an increasing reliance upon them. Each time you notice trust increasing you may still feel cautious.

Stage 4: Rely on the Other Person Functionally

You begin to "do life" together again in whatever way you did before. Life tasks (e.g., scheduling with your spouse, managing projects with a coworker, going to social events with a friend) begin to be reinstituted. But the tone of these engagements is more functional than mutually enjoyable and free. The dissatisfying nature of this arrangement can often discourage continued growth (e.g., "I don't want to work this hard at trusting out of a sense of duty"), but this discouragement can be alleviated by understanding where it falls in the process of trust restoration. This is only stage 4 of 10.

Stage 5: Share Facts

As you functionally do life with this person, there is the opportunity for you to begin to share. To this point you have been receiving information more than giving information. Now, you begin the process of "giving yourself" again. You allow yourself to be known at a factual level. Questions from the other person that start with "why?" or "how come?" are still met with defensiveness. Questions that start with "would you?" become more comfortable as you allow this person to influence the facts (e.g., schedule) of your life again.

Stage 6: Share Beliefs

Becoming more comfortable sharing facts again naturally leads into sharing what you think about those facts. Conversations become more meaningful as you share more of what you like, dislike, agree with, disagree with, and want from the events of life. You can now talk about the way you believe things "should" be without a tone of judgment, sadness, or guilt overpowering the conversation. As you share your beliefs, you feel more understood. At this stage, you and the other person may have to learn or relearn how to have different opinions or perspectives without getting defensive.

Stage 7: Share Feelings

Up until this point in the process, emotions have likely been "thrust at" or "shown to" more than shared with the other person. At this level of trust, you are willing to receive support, encouragement, or empathy toward your emotions. You are beginning to experience your burdens being reduced and your joys multiplied as you share them with this friend. Friendship is beginning to feel like a blessing again.

Stage 8: Rely on Your Friend Emotionally

You are able to believe your friend is being transparent and sincere when they tell you about their day or share their feelings with you. It is now the exception to the rule when suspicions arise within you about your friend's motive for saying or doing something. Most interactions with your friend are now an "emotional net win"; that is, you feel better because of the interaction.

Stage 9: Allow Your Friend to Care for You

Allowing your friend to be kind or express appreciation has lost any sense of being unsafe, unwanted, or manipulative. When your friend wants to serve you, you no longer think they are doing an act of penance or setting you up for a request. How your friend hurt you is no longer the interpretative center point of the relationship. Your friend's efforts to bless you can be received as blessings rather than being treated as riddles to be solved.

Stage 10: Relax and Feel Safe with Your Friend

This is trust restored. Your friend's presence has become a source of security rather than a pull toward insecurity. Your friend's presence reduces stress in troubling circumstances. You find yourself instinctively drawn to your friend when something is difficult, upsetting, or confusing. Even when they don't have the answer, their presence is its own form of relief and comfort.

TRUST AND TIMETABLES

There is intentionally no pacing guide for this trust progression, which doesn't always arrive at stage 10. In that regard, growing in trust requires trust. It is an act of faith not to say, "I'll give it three months, and if we're not at stage 7, then I don't think there's any hope." That kind of time-pressured environment stifles the growth of trust.

Your goal in reading this progression is merely to gain an understanding of where you are and what is next in the development of trust. Efforts at artificially accelerating the process will ultimately do more harm than good. If you know where you are and what's next, you have the information you need to gauge when your friend's actions warrant you to begin taking the next step in wise trust.

QUESTIONS FOR REFLECTION

1. As you look over this trust progression, does there seem to be a large leap between any of the steps? If so, what stages would you add to balance the growth of trust between each step?
2. How does having a list like this help to make trust less all-or-nothing? How does the fear-inducing nature of an all-or-nothing approach to trust make it harder to trust?

Chapter 14

CRISIS AND POSTCRISIS FORGIVENESS

Too often we only think of the initial declaration of forgiveness. There is good reason for this. Forgiveness is hard. Forgiveness is powerful. When forgiveness is granted, it is a meaningful event. But if we only think of the event, we miss the stages of forgiveness that emerge with the passing of time.

Consider the following offenses that merit forgiveness:

- A spouse has been unfaithful with your best friend.
- A spouse hides a major amount of debt and jeopardizes many life dreams.
- A teenager "borrows" the car without asking and wrecks it.
- A friend shares your damaging secret.

When we play these situations out in our mind, we rehearse the moment of discovery, the process of learning how bad the offense was, tense preforgiveness conversations as we express hurt, and finally getting to the place of saying, "I forgive you." These all capture the *crisis* phase of forgiveness. During this time, alarms are blaring in our mind and heart. Time is moving fast.

If our life were a movie, the words "I forgive you" would be the climax; the postclimactic part of the script would be relatively short. Oh, if only life were a movie! Initial forgiveness is hard—something we wonder if we will ever be able to do. But *postcrisis* forgiveness is equally hard because it is the way of *endurance*—an exhausting endeavor that is quite comparable to the intensity of crisis-phase forgiveness.

THE STRUGGLE CONTINUES

After declaring, "I forgive you," we battle with fear, anger, mistrust, shame, and intrusive thoughts. Forgiving was so daunting we thought finally doing it would make our life easier. But then we realize, after an initial time of relief, postcrisis forgiveness is only a different kind of heavy. Crisis forgiveness was, in many ways, easier. It was heroic. It was focused. It forced us to our knees in reliance upon God's strength. Postcrisis forgiveness comes when we are grace-weary. It is mundane. It must cover a multitude of (comparably smaller) sins, not just one big sin. It can easily be distracted by so many things we are trying to catch up on (things that were neglected during the crisis phase).

During postcrisis forgiveness, when we offend (even if in lesser ways) the person we forgave, we are now the one to repent. Everyday irritants call for patience and grace, but we feel like we have been gracious and patient enough. Our spouse, child, or friend offends us again—perhaps forgetting to follow through on a commitment—and we are called to relate to them independent of the original offense.

Postcrisis forgiveness calls us to appreciate the incarnation as much as the crucifixion. In addition to becoming sin for us (2 Corinthians 5:21), Christ came and lived among us for more than three decades filled with many ordinary days and common conflicts. Christ lived in the midst of our sin, in a fallen broken world with selfish, manipulative, backstabbing friends. Postcrisis forgiveness calls us to emulate Jesus incarnationally living with those whose sin he would forgive.

Too often we (the forgiver) assume that the restoration process will go directly from forgiveness to peace. There is a reciprocal fallacy of the forgiven person when they assume they will move directly from forgiven to trusted. However, especially when the offense being forgiven profoundly disrupted life, there is a middle stage. If we forget this, we may wrongly assume that we have failed to forgive when we meet these new challenges. Rather, it means that we have moved to a new stage of restoration—from canceling the debt to restoring trust.

Saying that there is sometimes a middle stage to restoration does not change the necessity or requirements of forgiveness. Nor does it allow the one being forgiven to rush or demand quicker restoration. It does remind us that the Bible is more than a collection of commands. It is a portrait of our complete life experience captured in the person of Christ. With every struggle we face, we have the opportunity to marvel at a new feature of Jesus's character and begin the process of emulating that quality.

Postcrisis forgiveness—which simply means walking out the implications of forgiveness in mundane moments and exhibiting grace during those moments—is a chance to appreciate the gritty commonness of Christ's humanity and to realize Jesus lived these moments perfectly, too, both to redeem our shortcoming in these moments and as our example of honoring God in the midst of them.

Don't let the new challenges of postcrisis forgiveness unsettle you. In many ways, this chapter has been like talking to a preteen about puberty. You don't tell a preteen about the changes of puberty and then say, "Do it." Education about puberty is not about implementation. You have the conversation, so the young person is not unsettled by the changes and is comfortable talking to you about them.

That is the purpose of this chapter. We can't make postcrisis forgiveness easy. We can raise awareness that it presents new challenges. We can open the conversation so that, when these new challenges emerge, you have words for it instead of assuming that you or the other person are necessarily doing something wrong.

QUESTIONS FOR REFLECTION

1. Can you think of an example in your life when postcrisis forgiveness was more difficult than crisis-phase forgiveness?
2. What are other challenges, not mentioned in this chapter, that emerge during postcrisis forgiveness, which are often overlooked and, therefore, catch us by surprise?

Chapter 15

REMEMBERING WELL AFTER FORGIVENESS

What do we do with our memories after we forgive? We wish Morpheus from the *Matrix* would offer us the blue pill that allows blissful ignorance of the offense that is sticky in our minds because it is associated with so many events, people, and places that are important to us. But in the absence of that possibility, we must learn to remember well after forgiving.

FOUR SEQUENTIAL ASPECTS OF REMEMBERING WELL

1. Remembering Well Means Remembering Accurately

Accurate memory helps us understand ourselves at a deeper level and respond to our emotions more wisely. We naturally realize that events impact emotions. It is less intuitive, and often a point of defensiveness, to acknowledge how emotions shape memories. Remembering accurately means we can create a list of the things that were said and done and a corresponding list of the things that we felt in response.

We will never be able to separate emotions from the experience. This is an artificial, yet still important, distinction. Emotions are a part of our experience. But we can strive to understand which parts of our memory were modified, exaggerated, muted, deemed irrelevant, or made central because of our emotions during an experience. This helps us do the next thing.

Forgiveness does not revise history. God is the God of truth. Much of the Bible is the recording of historical events, many of which were epically sinful actions of God's people. God does not say to us, "Just pretend like that bad thing never happened."

As we seek to remember accurately (something we will never do perfectly), we need to begin to differentiate events from emotions. Both are real. Both are important. Each influences the other. Metaphorically, if you imagine a movie, events are what you see on the screen and the words the actors say. Emotions are the soundtrack playing in the background that adds depth to the actions and words.

2. Remembering Well Means Remembering Wisely

We remember in order to be able to respond. History teachers like to say, "Those who do not study history are doomed to repeat it." Initially, it should be self-evident that we remember to respond wisely to the person who hurt us. That is why we've spent several chapters on proportional trust and examining how wise trust develops.

But remembering wisely doesn't only prepare us to respond to the person who hurt us. *Remembering accurately also helps us respond wisely to our future reactions.* Remembering wisely allows us to identify many things:

- We identify things we could have never known. This helps us let go of false guilt.
- We identify things that raised concerns, but we chose not to respond to them. This helps us be wiser in future, similar situations.
- We identify ways our current responses are heightened or muted now. This helps us understand when our emotions

are more rooted in the then-and-there than the here-and-now, which helps us respond wisely to the present while healthily mourning the past.

Additionally, *remembering accurately helps us respond to God wisely.*

- Misremembering makes a mess of emotions like guilt, shame, and regret. These are emotions we naturally bring to God. The less accurate we are in assigning these emotions to a situation, the more it interferes with our relationship with God.
- Misremembering impairs our ability to receive God's comfort. Often, we try to repent for things that were not our fault. This gives us the sense that, when life is hard, God sees us with condemnation rather than compassion.
- Misremembering makes the application of the Bible feel dangerous. If we enact good, biblical principles in situations for which they were not intended, they do not work. This makes the situation worse. We begin to feel like God and the Bible failed us.

3. Remembering Well Means Remembering Gracefully (with Grace)

Calling bad things bad (remembering accurately) and increasing our situational or self-awareness (remembering wisely) are not punitive, although a person who is not fully repentant will often claim that it is. Remembering gracefully means we want the person who hurt us to know both the full *conviction* and full *forgiveness* of God for their sin.

The first part of this is easy. We want the person who hurt us to experience conviction. If our desire stops there, however, we are not remembering gracefully. Remembering gracefully does not revoke any precaution that remembering wisely entails. Remembering gracefully does not require foolish trust, but it does mean desiring that Christ would redeem every sinner (including the one who hurt us).

Where does that start? It begins by being able to say, "My experience of heaven would not be tarnished by their presence. I will resist the impulse to make God choose between me or them." While we don't have that power, we can take that emotional stance. Next, remembering gracefully can choose not to be resentful of good things that occur in the life of the person who hurt us. Actually, this gives the person who hurt us less power over our life and is, thereby, liberating for us.

Where does it go from there? As every counselor says, "That depends." It goes as far as wise trust (see chap. 14) deems appropriate, at the pace of your healing and restoration.

4. Remembering Well Means Remembering with Hope

Some of us get overwhelmed at the idea of remembering gracefully because we feel rushed. This is where hope comes in. We don't need hope for a finished journey. A college student does not say, "I hope I graduate high school."

Hope means an important road is ahead and that we believe, with God's strength, we will eventually complete that part of our journey (Philippians 1:6). Remembering with hope means we do not give the darkness of past pain the final word on our life. Remembering with hope means we believe the light ahead is brighter than the darkness behind.

Remembering with hope trusts that God will wipe away every tear in heaven (Revelation 21:4) and looks for the ways in which God is proving himself good in the land of the living (Psalm 27:13). Remembering with hope has the courage and integrity to be honest about our doubts. It brings those doubts to someone we trust, God, for reassurance. That is what every psalm of lament does.

Now you may say, "I get it. This is helpful. But it's incomplete. It's not enough." You are right. If remembering well is where you are stuck, I would recommend the book *The End of Memory* by

Miroslav Volf.[1] Miroslav writes about his experience of forgiving "Captain G," his chief interrogator for eight years while a political prisoner for being a Christian and "Western sympathizer" in the former communist Yugoslavia. He provides an excellent, sensitive, and gospel-centered consideration of what to do with profoundly painful memories after forgiving.

QUESTIONS FOR REFLECTION

1. Before reading this chapter, if someone asked you what they were supposed to do with painful memories after they've forgiven the person who hurt them, what would you have said?

2. Which of the four aspects of remembering well captures where you are in dealing with painful memories after forgiving? If you have forgiven multiple intensely painful experiences, you may be at a different place with each one.

---

1. To read an excerpt from Volf's *The End of Memory*, "Memories after Forgiveness: A Series from Miroslav Volf (Part 1 of 7)," bradhambrick. com, March 23, 2015, http://bradhambrick.com/volf1/.

Section 4:
Embracing Forgiveness
from Others

Most of this book has been about navigating the emotional, relational challenges of extending forgiveness. But we don't reside only on the offended side of the forgiveness equation. We also reside on the offender side. Our sin also needs to be forgiven, by God and by those we hurt.

Guilt can be as sticky as pain. Seeing the pain in someone else's eyes can be as disruptive as feeling the pain in your own chest. Forgiveness can be as difficult to embrace as it is to dispense. That is why we will devote this section to understanding how to respond to the challenges of embracing forgiveness.

Chapter 16

IS EMBRACING FORGIVENESS FROM PEOPLE HARDER THAN FROM GOD?

It is one thing to live forgiven in the eyes of God. It is something else to live forgiven in the eyes of another person. Just because an offense against a perfect God is more significant does not mean embracing God's forgiveness is more difficult.

We must not allow the ultimate significance of embracing God's forgiveness to cause us to miss the challenges of embracing forgiveness from other people. We must not be deceived into thinking that we have greater reverence for God's forgiveness by downplaying the things that are uniquely hard when forgiveness is exchanged between people.

Here are five challenges inherent in embracing forgiveness from another person—challenges that do not exist when we embrace God's forgiveness.

1. WE SEE THE PEOPLE WE OFFEND

We don't see the expression on God's face. We don't hear the tone or pain in God's voice. We don't see God at church, notice he walks into another room, and wonder if he is avoiding us. We don't send God a text message and in every moment he doesn't reply wonder whether this is an indication of how upset he is.

These realities create more stimuli for us to process as we embrace forgiveness from another person. It is one thing to differentiate the sound of a flute from a clarinet. It is another thing to pick out the sound of each while a full orchestra is playing. The amount of visual, auditory, and affective (i.e., emotional) information that bombards us when we are seeking to embrace the forgiveness of another person is greater than when we embrace God's forgiveness.

2. PEOPLE ARE MORE HARMED BY OUR SIN THAN GOD IS

God is durable and sturdy. We don't worry about doing irreparable damage to God. The offense of sin is against his holiness. Sin is as inadmissible in God's presence as trying to touch two polarized magnets. Sin offends God and creates distance from him, but now that the work of Calvary is complete, sin doesn't hurt God. He does not live in perpetual pain because we continue to sin. God is saddened and offended by our sin, but he does not wince in pain.

With God, we only face the reality of our sin. In God's perfect fatherly-ness, he keeps the focus on what needs to change. With other people, we face the consequences our sin has on them. Sin wounds people physically, relationally, emotionally, or spiritually. We can see the pain we caused. This is often distracting and overwhelming. Even after being forgiven, we see the person carry the load we created. This is different than when we know God rejoices in the opportunity to forgive (Luke 15:7).

3. PEOPLE HAVE NOT PROMISED FORGIVENESS AHEAD OF TIME

We come to God knowing he has already promised, "If we confess our sins, he is faithful and just to forgive us our sins and to cleanse us from all unrighteousness" (1 John 1:9). We know that Jesus has already cried out in victory, "It is finished" (John 19:30). We ask

God for forgiveness already knowing the answer. We do not worry about God changing his mind.

We ask people for forgiveness with a sense of suspense. They may say, "I need time," or worse, "No." They may ask clarifying questions to make sure we understand what we did, whereas God already knows our hearts. They may ask for consequences of our sin to be amended (e.g., telling a mutual friend what we said about them was untrue). The uncertainty of being able to answer "What if they . . ." questions is often what inhibits us from seeking forgiveness.

4. PEOPLE ARE NOT PERFECT AT FORGIVING

For God, forgiveness is not a process or a journey. The only process involved in God's forgiveness is our sanctification. God never comes back and says, "You know, I thought I had forgiven you, but . . . " and explains a new aspect of his pain he just came to know. God doesn't claim to forgive and then continue to be passive-aggressive. There are no other gods who have "done us this way" and left us wondering if the real God will also, like other people who claim to have forgiven us but continued to hold our offense over our head.

When we seek forgiveness, two people are midjourney: us, putting our sin to death; and our friend, learning to forgive. When we embrace forgiveness from another person, we must leave space for them to be midjourney too. God is perfect and therefore doesn't need to grow from the experience of forgiving. With people, we are both growing. This can be messy. Embracing forgiveness from another person requires that we be willing to enter this messiness with them as they have been willing to enter it with us.

5. PEOPLE TAKE TIME TO HEAL

Jesus literally bore the sins of the world at Calvary, and it only took him three days to fully recover. While Jesus was bearing the sins of the world, he was able to pray, "Father, forgive them, for they know not what they do" (Luke 23:34). With God, forgiveness is purely on our timeline.

With another person, forgiveness may be delayed because of healing that needs to occur in their life. The other person did not choose for us to hurt them. We cannot choose the pace at which they forgive. When forgiveness is delayed as the other person takes time to heal, we are forced to face the magnitude and impact of our sin. Rushing our friend is a form of minimizing our sin.

The fact that it's messier to be forgiven by people than by God should make us more grateful for God's forgiveness. It should deepen our appreciation for many of the attributes of God that make our salvation (i.e., restoring right relationship with God) straightforward.

It should also deepen our empathy and compassion for those we sin against. We should resist the urge to expect them to be like God in how they forgive us. We realize the importance of patience—allowing them to forgive at their own pace.

This glimpse at the messiness of the forgiveness process should also help us articulate some of the challenges we face if we are the one forgiving. Even when our forgiveness is slow, we can love the person we want to forgive by putting into words the strain that exists. Mutual understanding and patience create an environment of love and trust that allows forgiveness to be cultivated.

QUESTIONS FOR REFLECTION

1. Think of a time when forgiveness was difficult for you to embrace. Which of the challenges listed in this chapter capture the barriers you were trying to navigate?

2. How has this chapter increased your appreciation for the attributes of God that make embracing his forgiveness simple?

Chapter 17

FORGIVENESS AND SHAME, NOT JUST GUILT

Shame is one of the obstacles to experiencing the emotional free-dom that forgiveness should bring. We often treat guilt and shame as synonyms, as if saying "guilt and shame" is the equivalent of saying "water damage and moisture damage." But the experiences of guilt and shame are not the same thing.

If you have done much reading about guilt and shame, then you know they have a myriad of distinctions. Actually, there are so many distinctions that it can get confusing and you begin to wonder, "Which distinction is right?" But this reflection will err on the side of simplicity. In this chapter we will say guilt focuses on what we did and shame focuses on who we are.

Guilt feels the weight of having done a bad thing. Guilt is about activity. The worse the bad thing done, the greater the weight felt. Guilt knows there are consequences for the bad thing and is concerned with how to resolve those consequences.

Shame believes what we have done makes us less than. There are no degrees of consequence with shame; rather, there is the inherent sense of being unacceptable. Shame is about identity.

Even though forgiveness cancels a debt, shame makes us feel like we won't be admitted into the store to buy something even if we had the money.

SHAME, FORGIVENESS, AND GOD

We begin to see that forgiveness alone is not enough. A defendant in a court case can be forgiven for their crime (guilt: penalty canceled) only to come home and not be welcome there (shame: deemed unacceptable). The gospel speaks to both guilt and shame. The gospel offers *propitiation* (penalty-bearing sacrifice) for guilt and *adoption* (full inclusion into God's family) for shame.

A good picture of God addressing shame is in Psalm 3. King David's myriad of sinful choices has led to the destruction of his family. Failing to address one son raping his daughter has led to another son killing his brother. Seeing his father's unresponsiveness leads that son to start a military coup to oust his father. This is why David is running for his life.

When we wreck our family, we don't just feel guilty. We also feel ashamed. In Psalm 3, writing about his encounter with God, David reveals that he was feeling shame and how God addressed his shame. David declares that God is "the lifter of my head" (v. 3). If David were feeling guilt, he would have said "the washer of my stain" or "the bearer of my penalty." Both of these statements are true, but they would not have addressed what David was experiencing.

It can be said that shame is an "experience of the eyes." A child who feels inferior (ashamed) at school will avoid eye contact with teachers and peers alike. To make and hold eye contact is an indication we feel equal to the other person. This is why when training a puppy, the master stares into the puppy's eyes until the puppy looks away. It establishes the roles of master and pet.

David felt shame; his eyes were on his sandals. He wasn't only head-drooping sad but eye-contact-avoiding ashamed. God's response was to gently put his hand under David's chin and draw

David's gaze to God's tender eyes of grace. Loving eye contact did what the verbal contract "I forgive you" never could.

If you read the Bible with this point of awareness, you will begin to notice passages that speak about the gospel emphasize that we are both forgiven (the remedy for guilt) and accepted (the remedy for shame) because of what Christ did on our behalf. We need to be proficient in articulating both if we are going to embrace and minister the gospel fully.

SHAME, FORGIVENESS, AND OTHERS

This chapter is only skimming the surface of what could be written on the topic of shame. Here we will only deal with shame for sins we committed; hence, forgiveness is relevant. We will not deal with the shame we feel for sins committed against us (such as abuse). Shame emanating from suffering receives a different form of comfort and has a different healing process.[1]

We return to the dilemma that things are often easier with God than they are with other people. As we saw in the last chapter, God is durable, ever ready, consistent, and always receptive for us to engage. With God, it is only our readiness to receive that is in question, not his readiness to give. People are different.

We think now of parents whose addiction made them utterly unreliable for their children. We think of the business or ministry leader who was fired for embezzling money. We think of the spouse who committed adultery. We realize simply hearing the words, "I forgive you," doesn't make eye contact comfortable, natural, or, sometimes, even appropriate. The debt may be canceled and, even if the other person is not being punitive, there can be major obstacles to a restored relationship.

As the offender, we wonder, "What is my relational standing?" This is where conversations often get dicey. We should remember

1. For more on this, see "Shame: 4 FAQ's—Shame vs. Guilt or Regret? Words to Speak? Resources? Counseling?," bradhambrick.com, September 7, 2018, http://bradhambrick.com/ShameSermon/.

that forgiveness does not mean the removal of consequences. A child can be forgiven for hitting a baseball through the window and still be expected to pay for the window. We should remember that trust still builds wisely over time. So acceptance does not mean removal of consequences or full trust instantly.

Acceptance simply means, "We are equals. We are of the same kind. I am not enforcing social dominance over you because of your sin against me." It may be a journey for the forgiving person to get to this place. Again, we must leave room for them to be midjourney too.

What do we do if shame is a barrier in our ability to embrace the forgiveness that someone has given? What if they are willing, but we are impeded by shame? Although it might be awkward, we could ask for a conversation like the one below. During this conversation, each person would be intentional about maintaining eye contact.

> *You:* [acknowledge the wrong of what I did, accepting any ongoing consequences of wise trust]

> *Person You Hurt:* [express forgiveness again] Then, "I want you to know that while what you did was wrong, it does not make you 'less than.' I not only forgive you as Jesus forgave me; I accept you as God accepts us."

> *You:* "Thank you." [the two of you mutually look away]

In future interactions, you are mindful not to avoid eye contact. If your friend notices you are avoiding eye contact, they can take this as an indication that shame may be reemerging and say some version of, "You are not less than. There is no need to look away."

The behavioral residue (i.e., habits that emerge from our emotions) of shame can become a deeply ingrained habit. Having the people who love us invite tender eye contact as they remind us of the simple truth of acceptance can be a powerful counter to this habituation.

QUESTIONS FOR REFLECTION

1. In your own words, what is the difference between guilt and shame? How does the gospel address each in a unique way?
2. Give an example of when tender eye contact made a profound difference in a moment when you were experiencing shame?

Chapter 18

THE OFFENSIVENESS OF GOD FORGIVING SINS AGAINST ME

I once thought that because forgiveness was "nice" and "good" that it must be "pleasant" and couldn't be "hurtful." I remember the blissfulness of that ignorance. The world was a simpler place then. But two things opened my eyes to the reality that there was more to the story.

The first thing was being a counselor. Counselors spend their workweek hearing stories of advanced brokenness—stories of abuse, trauma, and betrayal. Neat answers don't fit these jagged situations. There was no reasonable assurance that if we do what you're supposed to do the other person will follow suit. There was a need to add cautious wisdom to the virtue of forgiveness. But was that okay? I felt like I needed permission to ask necessary questions.

The second thing gave me this permission. Rereading *Mere Christianity*, I came upon these words:

> [Jesus] told people that their sins were forgiven, and never waited to consult all the other people whom their sins had undoubtedly injured. He unhesitantly behaved as if

He was the party chiefly concerned, the person chiefly offended in all offenses. This makes sense only if He really is the God whose laws are broken and whose love is wounded in every sin.[1]

What C. S. Lewis did best, in my opinion, was to ask the Christian faith to answer real, honest questions. He put uncomfortable things into words. He made them acceptable to talk about. He wasn't a rebel or being irreverent. He was just honest and vulnerable. If God was real and the Bible was true, he thought it was fair to ask honest questions. That was the permission I needed.

AN UNCOMFORTABLE TRUTH

With that in mind, let's continue to engage hard questions about forgiveness. Imagine the same thief robbed you and a friend. Perhaps you were together at the state fair and were robbed at the same time. The thief was caught and brought before you. Your friend speaks first and says, "*We* forgive you." How does that make you feel?

Chances are, you're offended. Even if you were willing to forgive, you don't like someone speaking for you. More than a loss of voice, it doesn't seem right for someone else to forgive on your behalf. It wouldn't matter if the thief stole twice as much from your friend. Your debt wasn't their debt to cancel. So, we ask, is that what God does when he forgives sins that also offended or harmed us?

The answer is yes and no. Yes, God forgives the sins committed against me without my consent. I can choose not to forgive, but the person who offended me can get into heaven and have emotional rest in their standing before God.

No, God does not forgive *for* me (meaning, in my place or usurping my voice). The possibility exists for God to cancel the debt toward him, and I do not cancel the debt toward me. In which case,

---

1. C. S. Lewis, *Mere Christianity* (New York: Harper Collins, 2003), p. 51–52.

God warns me about misunderstanding the extent to which I have been forgiven (Matthew 18:21–35). By being an example, Jesus creates social pressure for those who identify with him—people who call themselves Christians.

This is where we get uncomfortable. We feel rushed. God is a patient shepherd who walks at the pace of his sheep. But we don't like the predetermined direction. We don't like the truth that Christians must forgive. We want to be followers of Jesus; we just don't want him to be "out front."

Most of our resistance is that we do not want to be put in harm's way by forgiving. In previous chapters, we already talked through the progression of wise trust, that manipulative repentance does not fool God, and reasons to withhold steps toward restoration. We've established that God is patient and forgiveness is a process.

This can all be true, but our heart still grumbles. Why? Because there is a degree of satisfaction in anger and bitterness. Often, these emotions feel like the only thing we have left to commemorate our pain. Releasing these emotions feels like erasing history, like tearing down a monument to a horrific event. Remember, you will always have healthy grief over these events, even when you surrender to anger. Frederick Buechner comments on the satisfaction and effect of anger:

> Of the seven deadly sins, anger is probably the most fun. To lick your wounds, smack your lips over grievances long past, roll over your tongue the prospect of bitter confrontation still to come, to savor to the last toothsome morsel both the pain you are given and the pain you are giving back—is a feast fit for a king. The chief drawback is that what you are wolfing down is yourself. The skeleton at the feast is you.[2]

---

2. Frederick Buechner, *Wishful Thinking: A Theological ABC* (New York: Harper & Row, 1973), 2.

This is a reality that we must grapple with. We must admit, we often enjoy being angry. It feels powerful. It feels right. When we were hurt, we felt powerless and voiceless. Anger feels like the antidote to these experiences. The call to forgive feels like a call backward rather than a move forward. This is why it bothers us for Jesus to be out front.

Regardless of how patient our Good Shepherd is, we must come to trust his direction and example. Early in our journey, it is enough to know that he is patient and understanding. "Actions" toward forgiveness feel a long way off. Once we get to the point where it feels reasonable for forgiveness to be imminent, we can begin to dislike Jesus's example.

But like every other emotional challenge we've faced on this journey, our pattern remains the same: put into words what is hard so we can have an honest conversation with God and others. Conversation with a friend and prayer with God prevents us from feeling alone in the challenge of obedience.

QUESTIONS FOR REFLECTION

1. Have you ever found it odd that God forgives the sins that were committed against you? When did this strike a chord of discomfort with you?

2. What are the things that make it most difficult for you to surrender anger over a past hurt? Maybe it is not the same thing for every hurt. If not, what has made it hard to surrender anger in the offenses that have been most difficult for you to forgive?

Section 5:
Moving toward What
Is Commonly Called
"Closure"

Sitcoms come to conclusion in thirty minutes. Movies take about two hours. Novels require two hundred to three hundred pages. Sermons . . . well . . . that varies from church to church, and I won't guess, but it's usually less than an hour. Forgiveness doesn't come with a time stamp. It is a story that unfolds, a journey to traverse, and a life to live.

While we don't want to be rushed to forgive, we also don't want to live indefinitely with the heavy baggage of unforgiveness. This section explores what we commonly call "closure," although we'll offer an alternative category. The goal is to help you travel toward forgiveness efficiently, without rushing you. We want to help you see the good fruit of forgiveness, even when forgiving doesn't mean things are "all better." If you find yourself saying, "I can't do that," add the word "yet" to the end of the sentence. Don't feel rushed. Continue your journey from where you are.

Chapter 19

FORGIVENESS AND EMOTIONAL FREEDOM

As we think about how forgiveness contributes to emotional freedom (i.e., not having a past offense determine your present emotions), we must debunk a common and understandable misunderstanding about emotional freedom: It is not always pleasant, any more than personal freedom is always pleasant. We can live with personal liberty but have a life that is still hard. We can live with emotional freedom and our emotions can still be unpleasant. With that in mind, we will consider a few different aspects.

FIVE WAYS FORGIVENESS AND EMOTIONAL FREEDOM INTERRELATE

1. Emotional Freedom Exists on a Spectrum

Any emotional experience can be greater or lesser. You can be less mad or more mad. You can be less sad or more sad. In the same way, you can be less free, a little more free, quite a bit free, or very free.

As you gauge your growth toward emotional freedom, don't just measure it against where you would like to be and be discouraged that you're not there yet. Measure your growth from where you were and be encouraged by the progress already made. Both measures are needed—progress made (past) and progress to be made (future).

Emotional growth tends to occur like physical growth. You don't always notice it's occurring until you're surprised by how much it has occurred. As a child, every day felt about the same until you visited your grandparents and they marveled at how much you'd grown. Similarly, you don't feel yourself getting emotionally stronger until something happens that puts your growth on display.

Here we face the reality that unforgiveness is more noticeable than forgiveness. Anger and despair catch more attention than a proportional response. You will have to be intentional to notice the growth in emotional freedom that forgiveness brings. The next three points about emotional freedom provide examples of what you might notice.

2. Freedom Means the Absence of Mental Preoccupation

Before we forgive, the offense against us is central in our emotions. Practically, this means that a large number of events remind us of the offense. That is how memory works: association. I smell fresh cut grass, and I remember a baseball field because I associate that smell with that place. After the memory of baseball is activated, then memories of specific teammates or games come to mind.

It is hard to disassociate things from memories. But we can decentralize experiences. Now that I am a homeowner and a father, fresh cut grass is associated with chores and playing in the yard. Baseball is less central to my life, so the association is weaker (less central). Memories of baseball come to mind after memories of backyard camping, if at all.

Forgiveness means Christ's payment for sin is more central to how we remember our pain. When we remember a debt, we either remember it as "unpaid" or "paid." When we say, "I forgive you," we are declaring Christ "paid" that relational debt on that person's behalf. *There is emotional freedom in no longer tracking a debt.* But that is not the totality of our relationship with this person or their offense. To revisit the financial metaphor, continuing in relationship is to continue to "do business together" so there is still a metaphorical "line of credit" between us.

Wise trust means that this person's repentance is more central. Forgiveness gets the person from indebted to breakeven. That gives enough emotional freedom to begin living in the present moment. Then, as the fruits of repentance emerge, wise trust allows us to more fully live in the present.

In many ways, living fully in the present is what allows children to play. We marvel at their innocence and get jealous that "they don't have a care in the world." While adult responsibilities may not restore that childlike innocence, forgiveness gives us emotional freedom by allowing us to increasingly live in the present moment.

3. Freedom Means Responding to New Events on Their Own Merit

Imagine a friend lied to you. You rightly feel hurt. Chances are you don't only mistrust that friend; you also started to weigh the words of others more carefully. Part of the emotional load is the mistrust toward the friend who lied, but an equal (if not heavier) part of the load is a more generalized mistrust.

Forgiveness allows you to remove the lens of mistrust from the rest of life. As a result of being hurt, you will be less innocent than you were before. But less innocent does not have to mean mistrusting. You can be wisely cautious without being generally suspicious.

Let's use the example of children again. A child may innocently do a belly flop the first time they jump off a diving board. It hurts. Initially, the child mistrusts the water, diving boards, lifeguards, and everything else related to a swimming pool. Well processed, this experience teaches the child to be wise about how they enter the water. But being less innocent doesn't mean the inability to enjoy swimming or diving. This takes us to our next point.

4. Freedom Means the Ability to Engage New Tasks and to Take Wise Risks

One side effect of unforgiveness is a constriction in the number of emotional and relational risks we are willing to take. Often, the expression of anger associated with unforgiveness is an "allergic reaction" or "reflex response" to an interaction requiring some form of emotional or relational risk.

This is why living out forgiveness requires situational awareness and self-awareness. We need *situational* awareness to identify the interactions or activities that require some form of risk. For example, if the hurt was associated with rejection, the risk may be as simple as sharing our opinion. We need *self-awareness* to identify the internal response being masked by anger. Again, if the hurt was associated with rejection, the internal response might be embarrassment or insecurity.

Forgiveness is what allows us to enter this next phase of growth. It is this growth that often allows us to look back on significant hurt and say, "I am a stronger person for having gone through that." Too often that phrase is equated with, "What doesn't kill us makes us stronger," which is too generic and aloof. When we can identify and articulate the growth that occurred, it allows us to see the good thing God did during a hard time and, thereby, have our trust in God grown as well.

5. Emotional Freedom Is Comparable to Healthy Grief

We return to where we started—the reality that freedom doesn't always feel good. In this case, freedom feels like grief. Grief is when you accept that an unwanted thing has happened (for traditional grief, a death) and quit fighting against that reality. In many ways, denial is for grief-caused-by-death what anger is for grief-caused-by-offense.

Continuing the parallel, when you have grieved the death of a loved one, you still feel sad at times—perhaps the anniversary of their passing, their birthday, or Christmas when their seat at the table is empty. But this sadness doesn't control you, and it doesn't derail your ability to healthily engage the moment. You have assimilated their passing into your story, and you are continuing to live your story.

That is a good parallel for forgiveness. After you forgive, you still feel hurt at times. But this sense of hurt doesn't control you. You learn to healthily engage life even with the episodic distraction of feeling hurt. You assimilate the hurtful event(s) into your story and live the rest of your life without that event(s) having a controlling influence over your choices. That is what it means to be free.

QUESTIONS FOR REFLECTION

1. Prior to reading this chapter, how would you have defined emotional freedom and described its relationship to forgiveness?
2. With an offense that you are struggling to forgive (or was hard for you to forgive in the past), which of the five relationships between forgiveness and emotional freedom is most difficult to navigate?

Chapter 20

LOVE COVERS A MULTITUDE OF SINS

In his first epistle, the apostle Peter exhorts us, "Above all, keep loving one another earnestly, since love covers a multitude of sins" (1 Peter 4:8). What does it mean for love to cover a multitude of sins? How is this different from *covering up* (i.e., hiding or dismissing) sin?

Answering these questions will require us to get to know Peter and his audience better. If we approach this verse as a disconnected theological nugget, we are likely to misinterpret God's intent and, thereby, generate a sense of mistrust toward the God who calls us to forgive.

Read 1 Peter 4:1–8 and compare the suffering you experienced from an interpersonal offense with the suffering Peter's original audience is experiencing. Peter writes to Christian friends who were forced to leave their homes because of religious persecution (1 Peter 1:1).

Peter spends the first three chapters of this letter helping his friends process their experience of suffering—not just having to flee their homes but also experiencing unfair treatment in the places they settled afterward. As Peter begins to discuss love "covering a multitude of sins," he is building upon this encouragement and instruction.

Walking into verse 8, Peter is warning his exiled friends about the heightened temptations that come with intense suffering (1 Peter 4:1–4). He begins by reminding them that it is better to suffer than to sin (vv. 1–2). On a lesser scale of intensity, we teach our children the same thing: "Even if your friends make fun of you, it is important to do the right thing."

The Bible is realistic. Peter knew that when it feels like God has failed, it is easy to seek comfort or escape. That is why he makes a list of ways we often mentally and emotionally escape in hard times (1 Peter 4:3–4). When it is hard to believe we can cast our "anxieties on [God], because he cares for" us (1 Peter 5:7), we will often settle for a bottle, a lover, or rebellion against anything that represents the "order" that failed us.

Recognizing the powerful draw of this cynicism during suffering, Peter calls on these believers to be "self-controlled and sober-minded for the sake of your prayers" (1 Peter 4:7). When we suffer intensely, there is a strong tendency to *run from* something (e.g., the pain, the oppressor, or reality itself). Self-control is the opposite. It is *running to* something intentionally because you still have hope.

Without this kind of self-control, they would not pray. What happens when we don't pray? One result of prayerlessness is that we begin to expect from other people what only God can provide. We begin to expect the actions of people to be as satisfying and healing as the activity of God in our life. This has significant implications for forgiveness.

The repentance and efforts at making amends by those who hurt us will only be healing to a degree. There will always be a gap between what their contrition can do and the healing our heart needs. It may seem "fair" to hold them responsible for the gap. After all, they caused the pain, but doing so will leave us perpetually stuck in our pain. Remember, forgiveness is freedom for us too.

When we suffer intensely, our thoughts ride the wave of our circumstances and we take on a pattern of thinking, bracing against worst-case scenarios. Being sober-minded is different. When we are sober-minded, we weigh things rightly. Peter addresses the deep-seated skepticism that creeps in with suffering and unforgiveness. We begin to assume the worst as a form of self-protection. But the short-term protection that accompanies this kind of thinking comes at the price of long-term emotional pain and bondage.

It is from this flow of thought that Peter writes, "Above all, keep loving one another earnestly, since love covers a multitude of sins" (v. 8). In light of our discussion, we can begin to see that one of the implications of this is that forgiveness changes the dominant narrative. Any good movie has multiple plot lines. A "twist" in the movie is when we realize a subplot was really the main theme of the movie.

When that occurs, does the previous main theme become untrue? No. It just becomes of lesser importance to understanding the movie. The previous main theme is understood as it serves the main plot. That is one picture of what it means for "love to cover a multitude of sins." In a twist of forgiveness, what was the main plot of pain becomes a preface to the plot twist of grace. The pain doesn't become untrue; it just serves to highlight the main plot.

Peter's primary example of this love gives us a clearer picture of what he has in mind—"show hospitality" (1 Peter 4:9). Peter is picking an activity which identifies a time when the suffering of exiles would be most pronounced. When are homeless exiles most tempted to sin? When it's time to eat, and there is no food. When it's time to sleep, and there is no shelter.

What is the natural instinct in these moments? Isolate. Self-protect. Look out for your own. Is that understandable? Absolutely. What is its effect? It adds loneliness and isolation to persecution. The pain echoes. The reverberation of our pain rings like hollow bells in a forsaken land.

Hospitality covers these sins. Caring for others and allowing others to care for you takes what was the main plot of pain and isolation and in a twist makes it a subplot to grace and community. Not only is it emotionally effective, but it is also logistically wise for people to rally resources in hard times.

Let's circle back to forgiveness more directly. Unforgiveness is self-protective and isolating. Unforgiveness does with trust what exiles do with food during persecution. It hoards them. Does it make sense? Yes. Is it effective? Not really. Unless there is a plot twist and we begin to live hospitably in healthy relationships, our souls begin to shrivel. We can feel it.

In previous chapters, we have discussed what wise trust looks like. But we painted a map; we did not create a timeline. We were cautious not to rush you. In that sense, we were like a doctor treating an ankle injury, advising not to put more weight on it than the ankle could bear. When you reach this point in your journey, that same doctor is saying the risk of not putting weight on the ankle is greater than the risk of walking normally. That is not a contradiction. It is actually a compliment of your progress.

To come out of that metaphor and speak plainly, the risk of unforgiveness is a lonely life marked by mistrust. For a time, processing the pain (i.e., keeping weight off the ankle) is wise. After a while, it becomes a way of life that makes pain the dominant plotline of your life. Forgiveness is the plot twist that covers—reinterprets, not hides—the story of pain with a story of grace. Even if it is unwise to open the door of relationship to the person who hurt you, forgiveness opens the door of relationship for you toward others.

QUESTIONS FOR REFLECTION

1. How is "forgiveness covers sin by creating a plot twist that supersedes the pain caused" different from "forgiveness covers sin by hiding it or pretending it doesn't exist"?

2. How does pain being the forefront plotline in your life long-term create isolation? As you wrestle with forgiveness, how is it wise to weigh the risk of forgiveness against the isolating effects of unforgiveness?

Chapter 21

FORGIVENESS AND LEAVING ROOM FOR THE WRATH OF GOD

Many books and articles written on forgiveness focus on Romans 12:17–18, "Repay no one evil for evil, but give thought to do what is honorable in the sight of all. If possible, so far as it depends on you, live peaceably with all." Less often do they focus on Romans 12:19, "Beloved, never avenge yourselves, but leave it to the wrath of God, for it is written, 'Vengeance is mine, I will repay, says the Lord.'"

That is unfortunate. When this happens, we are not availing ourselves of the whole counsel of God, and, thereby, we are neglecting to give adequate guidance for instances when "so far as it depends on you" does not result in adequate resolution. What do we do when our best efforts to forgive still result in a dangerous or unresolved situation?

I am glad the Bible addresses this question. Albeit an awkward subject, it is good and needed. God's people would be unnecessarily vulnerable if the subject were not addressed. We need to be grateful for truths that help us navigate uncomfortable situations, even when the application of those truths does not make the situation pleasant.

We begin by acknowledging our best efforts are not enough, by themselves, to create reconciliation. We are only responsible for what we can control—hence the phrase, "so far as it depends as you." When we have done what we can, whatever sadness we feel for unreconciled relationships should be called *regret*, not *guilt*. We feel regret for things we wish were different. We feel guilt for things we should have done differently.

Next Paul recognizes the natural human impulse in these situations. When our efforts are inadequate to get what we want, we tend to lash out. This is why Paul writes, "never avenge yourselves." He knows us. If we are in an *abusive* situation, a counter-aggressive response would be dangerous. In a *nonabusive* situation, vengeful responses are ineffective and allow our actions to become a distraction from the real problem.

Finally, we come to the key phrase, "but leave it to the wrath of God." At first, this might come across as the mother saying to defiant children, "Just wait until your father gets home" (i.e., the final judgment). If Paul were writing to the unrepentant person, that would be the effect. But Paul isn't writing to the proverbial defiant children. Paul is writing, metaphorically speaking, to the exasperated mother who is at her wits' end and doesn't know what else to do or say.

Let's summarize how far we've come in this passage:

- Verse 17: Don't sin in response to sin.
- Verse 18: You are only responsible for what you can control.
- Verse 19a: Be wary of the temptation to respond in anger to your lack of control.
- Verse 19b: When your actions have done all they can, leave the person to God.
- Verse 19c: God promises to be just in his response to all sin, so live at peace.

We begin to realize several things. First, to get to the point that verse 19 describes, we must really love the person who hurt us. Casual relationships and minor offenses don't carry the emotional weight to make this full journey. Second, that means by the time we get to verse 19 in practice we are often more sad than mad. It is grief that causes us not to take this last step (v. 19b). Third, we don't want to "give up" on the person, so we are tempted to try to "force change."

So, we are left with at least three questions:

1. How do I know when I have done all that I can?
2. How do I enact verse 19 when the offender is dangerous or the offense is illegal?
3. How do I enact verse 19 when the offender is safe and the offense is only immoral?

WHEN HAVE I DONE ALL I CAN?

It always feels like we can give a little bit more. Once we've moved the line of what we are willing to accept two miles, what is another three feet? If Jesus gave his life for me, what is another two hundred dollars to my addicted friend? Why did I believe the last dozen tearful apologies and not this one too?

The first recommendation here is, don't make these kinds of decisions alone. "Where there is no guidance, a people falls, but in an abundance of counselors there is safety" (Proverbs 11:14). Get input from people whose character you trust and people who know the type of offense you're dealing with well. You want to identify when you are enabling destructive behavior in the other person.[1] Using a visual illustration, you want to identify when your gracious response is on "step 18" of forgiveness and the other person is refusing to take "step 2" of repentance and change.

We begin to see that "doing all you can" doesn't mean "you can't do more." It means "you've done enough to prove that this person is not committed to repentance and change." Think of it

---

1. For more guidance on how to identify and avoid enabling behaviors, see "Video: 10 Keys to Ensure Caring Is Helping," bradhambrick.com, April 21, 2014, http://bradhambrick.com/10keyshelping/.

like pulling the starter rope on a lawn mower. You do not have to pull until your arm falls off to have done all you can. There comes a point where you have pulled enough to know that pulling again is not going to make a difference. The problem is something other than the force and repetition of your pulls. You don't have to dislocate your shoulder to prove the point.

WHAT IF THE OFFENDER IS DANGEROUS OR THE OFFENSE IS ILLEGAL?

This is the question Paul answers in Romans 13:1–6.[2] In summary, Paul says, "This is why God instituted the legal system and civil authorities." When people do dangerous and illegal stuff, the godly response is to call the police. When people are abusive, it is God-honoring to get a restraining order.

But many people ask, "Isn't that punitive instead of loving?" The answer is, "No." It is loving in two ways. First, it limits the amount of damage this person can do—to themselves, their reputation, and others. Second, it is an attempt to wake them up to the severity of their actions.

Criminals (i.e., those who commit crimes) who get upset at people who call the police are being manipulative. The person who made the choice to call the police doesn't ruin someone's life. The person who made the choices that warranted calling the police disrupted their own life. Their life will not be on the path to wholeness until they can acknowledge this.

WHAT IF THE OFFENDER IS SAFE AND THE OFFENSE IS ONLY IMMORAL?

This is the question Paul answers in Romans 12:20–21. In effect, he says, "Don't get so caught up in being right that you can't be nice." Verse 19 clarifies that being "nice" doesn't mean being "naive." But

---

2. For more on how Romans 13:1–6 is an extension of Romans 12:14–21, see "Why We Should Always Teach Romans 12 with Romans 13," bradhambrick.com, March 11, 2016, http://bradhambrick.com/romans13/.

you do treat them with the basic kindness of a stranger in need. Paul's example was offering food to someone who was hungry.

What good does this do? Paul says it is like heaping burning coals on their head, which was an ancient metaphor for waking someone up. I, for one, am grateful for just an alarm clock.

If we are cruel or indifferent to the person we are "leaving to God," then our apathy can be used by them to justify their being obstinate. But our casual kindness undermines this excuse without putting us in a place of continued vulnerability. Removing the excuse that we're being "mean" or "heartless" is an effort (not guarantee) to "wake them up" to their need to change.

We must accept the reality that our best efforts at restoration will not always result in restoration. When this is the case, we must have the loving courage and resolve to "leave them to God," doing only what wise trust allows while being casually kind.

QUESTIONS FOR REFLECTION

1. Before reading this chapter, how would you have defined "doing all you can" in a strained relationship? How would you define it now?

2. What are the ways that you tend to get exasperated when healthy reconciliation is outside of your control? How do these prolong the destructive relational pattern and confuse where change needs to begin?

Chapter 22

FORGIVENESS AND PROTECTING OTHER VULNERABLE PEOPLE

When this chapter is relevant, it is excruciating. There is no way around it. No words of explanation, however accurate or practical, will make it more comfortable. Put yourself in these situations:

- You realize your spouse has been abusing the children and now need to call Child Protective Services.
- You dated a popular guy in the college ministry. He raped you. Now you need to call the police.
- You discover that the church's financial officer has been embezzling funds. Now you need to file a criminal report.
- You watch a med tech be careless in how he/she fills prescriptions at the hospital or pharmacy. You need to talk to the ethical board.
- You realize your son or daughter has been stealing their grandparent's pain medicine and selling it to other students at school. You need to call the principal.

These kinds of moments tear at our souls. We know there is a right thing to do. We don't want to do it. In our discomfort and dismay, we look for other options. Forgiveness is often the "break glass in case of emergency" concept that allows us to rationalize not doing what we know we need to do. After all, "It might be unforgiving if I did what needs to be done. I mean, I wouldn't want someone to report me."

Read through that previous paragraph again. It doesn't make logical sense to refrain from reporting these kinds of criminal offenses, but unfortunately, too often it makes emotional sense. When we don't feel good about doing what needs to be done, we can convince ourselves that this kind of thought process is coherent.

WHEN DISCOMFORT DISTORTS LOGIC

Let's track the thought process step by step. We'll walk through it using first-person pronouns (i.e., I, me, my) to help it feel more like the critical moments of decision.

1. I learn of awful actions by someone I know and care about.
2. I feel angry, despondent, sick, betrayed, etc. At this point, I am thinking of the people harmed.
3. I realize what needs to be done (contacting the authorities). I realize many lives will change if I do.
4. I feel intensely worse. I'm not just aware of what happened (past tense). *I realize I must make choices (present tense). My focal point begins to shift to the impact on the person who did wrong.*
5. Reasoning begins to mix with emotion. I realize my actions will have huge consequences.
6. I focus on the outcome of my choice to act. I begin to consider doing nothing.
7. *I feel less "involved" in the situation if I take the more passive road.*
8. My conscience beats me up for considering the possibility of doing nothing.

9. Forgiveness emerges as a Christian theme that helps me rationalize that doing nothing is a godly response.

10. My choice to do nothing protects the wrongdoer instead of the vulnerable under the guise of forgiveness.

Do you see the "fog of war" beginning to settle in about halfway through the list? The first part of our thought process makes sense, but a shift begins at step 4. Steps 9 and 10 are the outcomes that frequently make the news as scandals—"a person does profoundly bad things and those near them do nothing." We never thought we would be the person protecting the wrongdoer, especially not in the name of Jesus.

How does that happen? The key shift points are step 4 and again at step 7; hence, they are in italic text in the progression.

When we only hear of a tragedy, we tend to identify with the victim. We think about what it would be like to be the person who was harmed. At step 4 in this journey, we begin to identify with the wrongdoer. Our actions affect them. We will have to explain our actions. So the question we ask changes from, "How would I want this situation handled if I were the vulnerable one(s)?" to, "How would I want this handled if I were the guilty one?" That shift changes everything!

The shift in question at step 4 leads to the change in conscience at step 7. In most situations, we interpret an unpleasant reaction by our conscience as an indication that what we are considering is wrong. We think about lying. Our conscience flares. We reconsider.

In this case, our conscience goes off for both choices—speaking up and staying silent. We succumb to the "safest" logic (safe measured by a sense of self-protection): "If you don't know what you should do, it is better to do nothing." In some situations, this logic works. If you're unclear which of two items to purchase, it is usually wiser to wait. Keep your money until you're certain.

But this is a different kind of choice. Doing nothing isn't the equivalent of saving your money. Doing nothing leaves the vulnerable exposed. Trauma specialist Judith Herman, speaking to instances of abuse, says, "It is very tempting to take the side of the perpetrator. All the perpetrator asked is that the bystander do nothing. He appeals to the universal desire to see, hear, and speak no evil. The victim, on the contrary, asks the bystander to share the burden of pain. The victim demands action, encouragement, and remembering."[1]

This dynamic is true whenever the actions of one person endangers a more vulnerable person.

Instinctively, we know this. That is why our conscience will not release us to the passive option. That is why the ninth step in our progression is so important. We misuse the Christian concept of forgiveness to con our conscience into silence.

We categorize our passivity as the gracious, forgiving, or Christlike response to the sin of the wrongdoer. We trick our conscience to affirm our endangerment of vulnerable people as a virtue. All it takes is a flip of the question for this façade to fade.

- What if you were the child being abused?
- What if you were the next girl this guy asked on a date?
- What if you were one of the church members giving in faith?
- What if you were the next person in line at the pharmacy?
- What if you were the parent of a student buying pills at school?

When we identify with the vulnerable instead of the more personal (e.g., our friend, spouse, child), the notion of being passive toward sin no longer seems gracious or forgiving. It is revealed for what it truly is—dangerous and cowardly.

So, we ask, "How do we convince ourselves of this?" One more distortion often occurs at step 10. We insert the word *innocent* in place of *vulnerable*, and our theology tells us that no one is really innocent. We are all sinners.

---

1. Judith Herman, *Trauma and Recovery* (New York: Basic Books, 1997), p. 7–8.

It is true. We are all sinners. But it is not true that "innocent" and "vulnerable" are suitable synonyms in this sentence. We are just as sinful as the drunk driver who kills another driver in a wreck. But we are also more vulnerable when we drive on the road not knowing which drivers are sober and which are intoxicated. Our need for forgiveness does not cancel out our vulnerability on the road.

It seems right to conclude with Micah 6:8, "He [God] has told you, O man, what is good; and what does the Lord require of you but to do justice, and to love kindness, and to walk humbly with your God?" That is the point of this chapter.

We obey this passage by noting the order of the verbs: (1) do justice, (2) love kindness, and (3) walk humbly. When justice for the vulnerable needs to be done, that is our first commitment. There is no contradiction between doing justice and loving kindness, even when our discomfort in doing justice tempts us to think otherwise. We walk humbly knowing we are better than no one in the situation. It is just that, based on the information we have, we have a unique and active role to protect.

We can acknowledge the emotional tension between forgiveness and protecting the vulnerable. But we must realize that this tension is only in our emotions (i.e., we feel torn), not in what is right.

QUESTIONS FOR REFLECTION

1. Can you think of a situation where the concept of forgiveness was used to justify passivity toward protecting the vulnerable? How well does the ten-step progression of thought capture what happened in that situation?

2. How would you help someone who felt torn about protecting the vulnerable because the action they needed to take felt punitive (i.e., unforgiving) toward the wrongdoer?

Chapter 23

FORGIVENESS AND EMOTIONAL MATURITY: ROOT AND FRUIT

We are culminating our journey through forgiveness with this chapter; therefore, our goal is to be as concrete as possible in our description of closure. But "closure" is more a theater term than a good fit for describing the final stage of forgiveness.[1] A drama can have a "closing act," but forgiveness doesn't end anything. Both the forgiver and forgiven live on after forgiveness. That is why we will use the term *maturity* to capture what we're after.

The metaphor of maturity helps us understand the journey of forgiveness more accurately. We are always maturing. Even the wisest among us are always growing and understanding things better. Once a door is closed, it remains closed unless someone decides to reopen it. We need a metaphor that allows for perpetual growth.

If we look at a six-year-old who is trying to process their parents' divorce and say, "They are just not mature enough to understand what is going on," we are not criticizing the child. We are

---

1. I find that the term closure overpromises and underdelivers on the experience many (perhaps most) people have after forgiving a major offense. If closure works for you, however, don't feel compelled to change it.

acknowledging where they are. We are not rushing them. We are naming a challenge. But if the child grows up to be a forty-two-year-old who mismanages their finances and say, "They never matured," we are making a moral assessment.

The concept of maturity allows us to assess both what is *hard* about forgiveness (suffering) and *bad* about unforgiveness (sin). The concept has the elasticity to flex with where someone is on their journey with the pain that has been inflicted upon them.

We also don't want to reduce all of life to our subject of discussion. Forgiveness is only one part of the maturational journey God has us on. Our goal here is simply to accurately describe the role forgiveness plays in the emotional maturation process. Forgiveness is not the totality of emotional maturity, but it is an important piece. We want to understand its role better.

To do so, we will look at the two-way relationship between forgiveness and maturity: root and fruit.

FORGIVENESS AS THE ROOT OF MATURITY

When the roots of a plant are not healthy, the plant will not thrive. The plant does not get what it needs to continue to grow, mature, and produce fruit. The better we understand how unforgiveness impairs the roots of emotional maturity, the more motivated and equipped we will be to persevere in the difficult journey of forgiveness. Unforgiveness impairs the emotional maturation process in three ways.

First, unforgiveness stunts or delays maturity. We can easily be so distracted by how much energy and effort forgiveness requires that we fail to see how much energy and effort unforgiveness requires. The time and thought absorbed by unforgiveness is time that is not given to maturational development that otherwise would be occurring.

The time you have invested in this book is time that you have reclaimed for your own emotional health and maturity. In the same way that a plant needs minerals and nutrients, our emotional maturity needs the concepts and categories to aid us in responding to the hardships of life in healthy and God-honoring ways.

Second, unforgiveness locks us in the past. Unforgiveness doesn't just absorb time; it also diverts our focus. We become so consumed and disoriented by what *happened* that we can't give our full attention to what is *happening.*

Perhaps you remember being a student taking a test and fearing you would do poorly on. Your fear sped you up. You didn't take the time to read the directions well, so you missed questions you knew the answers to. That is a parallel to the distraction of unforgiveness.

The mature you would say, "Take your time. Read the directions carefully." Even as a student, you probably knew this. But the emotional disruption of fear had you so locked in the future (i.e., receiving a bad grade), you couldn't stay grounded in the present. Unforgiveness does the same kind of thing with the past.

Third, unforgiveness skews our judgment. Unforgiveness is more than an emotional experience; it is a way of interpreting the world. Even when you're in the present, the people and situations around you become skewed by the unresolved hurt that you feel.

To use another image, imagine you severely jammed your thumb. Someone tries to hand you a gallon of milk (an innocent gesture). You respond with fear and/or anger because holding the milk container would further hurt your injured thumb. The unresolved physical pain changed how you interpreted that action. Unforgiveness does the same kind of thing emotionally and relationally.

MATURITY AS THE FRUIT OF FORGIVENESS

Developing healthy roots is the first step toward producing healthy fruit. As roots become healthy, the rest of the plant can flourish in the ways that God intended. What are the indicators (i.e., fruit) that forgiveness is enabling us to live in the ways that God intended? Forgiveness facilitates emotional maturity in three ways.

First, forgiveness shows that our values have matured. Let's take the worst-case scenario first. Let's assume the person who offended us is still dangerous. Forgiveness and wise trust (which in this case would involve social distance) means that we have returned to making the choices that are best for our life instead of living in response to the other person. Forgiveness frees us to be intentional rather than reactive.

In the more common situations where long-term self-protection is not needed, forgiveness allows us to decentralize emotional safety from our decision making. No one thrives where safety is at the center of their decision-making. That's the climate of a war zone. Forgiveness allows love for others and God's purpose for our life to be at the center of our decision making again.

Second, forgiveness frees us to live in the present. We've all heard and probably given the advice, "Wherever you are, be all there." It's good advice, but it's hard to follow. Forgiveness is a key part of our emotional hygiene that puts us in a position to live according to this principle.

If you are a planner like me, you are probably thinking, "Isn't it wise to learn from the past to prepare for the future?" This is true, too. Forgiveness allows us to learn from the past instead of being haunted by it. Forgiveness allows us to prepare for the future instead of needing to control it. Forgiveness is a key part of keeping a healthy relationship among the past, present, and future.

Third, forgiveness removes the lens of pain. The more we forgive, the better we can see: "I can see clearly now the pain is gone. I can see all the obstacles in my way. Gone are the dark clouds that had me blind."[2] The fact that these are lyrics to such an iconic song shows how universal the experience of pain clouding our judgment is.

---

2. I took the liberty of changing the word rain to pain in Johnny Nash's song "I Can See Clearly Now" (Epic, 1972), https://genius.com/Johnny-nash-i-can-see-clearly-now-lyrics. I believe this word exchange is more than a rhyming-words replacement and is true to the intent of what the lyrics intended to communicate.

To describe life, the Bible uses the metaphor of a race with obstacles (Hebrews 12:1). The person who can see most clearly is the person who will navigate this race best. Removing the missteps we make because of generalized mistrust or leaking anger tripping us up is a key marker that we are maturing in the race of life. We regain the freedom to respond to each moment on its own terms.

A FINAL WORD

As we conclude this journey through forgiveness together, I would leave you with one word: *persevere.* None of us does forgiveness perfectly. Anyone who wrestled through this material honestly sees areas they need to grow (myself included). Don't be overwhelmed by how distant the destination seems. Be faithful in taking the next step. Remain confident that God is for you and with you on this journey.

QUESTIONS FOR REFLECTION

1. How would you describe the advantages of describing the culmination of forgiveness as "maturity" rather than "closure"?
2. Where have you most clearly seen these examples of "root" and "fruit" in your own efforts to forgive?

Section 6:
Avoiding Ministry Mishaps

This section addresses specific issues that pastors, counselors, and church leaders face as they help others on the hard journey of forgiveness. The focus shifts from speaking to the person forgiving or receiving forgiveness to how church leaders minister on the subject of forgiveness.

The sharper the scalpel, the surer the hand of the physician needs to be. Forgiveness is an action powerful enough to inspire a million novels. There may be no theme with which a minister of the gospel needs to be more sure-handed and tender than forgiveness.

Most of this book has focused on the ministry of private, personal conversation. This section considers public teaching ministry. Here, we will consider three common ministry mishaps. We will delve into the arena of hermeneutics (principles of interpreting the Bible) and homiletics (the practice of teaching and preaching the Bible). In addition, we will consider when forgiveness becomes a fixation in the mental health struggle of obsessive-compulsive disorder.

Chapter 24

WHEN DISCUSSING PARABLES ABOUT FORGIVENESS

Read the parable of the unforgiving servant from Matthew 18:21–35. As you read the parable, ask yourself what is missing from this story.

> Then Peter came up and said to him, "Lord, how often will my brother sin against me, and I forgive him? As many as seven times?" Jesus said to him, "I do not say to you seven times, but seventy-seven times. Therefore the kingdom of heaven may be compared to a king who wished to settle accounts with his servants. When he began to settle, one was brought to him who owed him ten thousand talents. And since he could not pay, his master ordered him to be sold, with his wife and children and all that he had, and payment to be made. So the servant fell on his knees, imploring him, 'Have patience with me, and I will pay you everything.' And out of pity for him, the master of that servant released him and forgave him the debt. But when that same servant went out, he found one of his fellow servants who owed

him a hundred denarii, and seizing him, he began to choke him, saying, 'Pay what you owe.' So his fellow servant fell down and pleaded with him, 'Have patience with me, and I will pay you.' He refused and went and put him in prison until he should pay the debt. When his fellow servants saw what had taken place, they were greatly distressed, and they went and reported to their master all that had taken place. Then his master summoned him and said to him, 'You wicked servant! I forgave you all that debt because you pleaded with me. And should not you have had mercy on your fellow servant, as I had mercy on you?' And in anger his master delivered him to the jailers, until he should pay all his debt. So also my heavenly Father will do to every one of you, if you do not forgive your brother from your heart."

Remember, parables are fictional stories told to illustrate a primary point. So, it's not heretical for us to ask the question, "What is missing?" We're not questioning Jesus. We're considering, "As Jesus made his primary point, what inferences might we make that would be unwarranted?" We honor Jesus's primary point by not applying it in ways that are a bad fit.

So, have you noticed what is missing yet? There are no rebuttals.

The first servant doesn't make excuses for why things "aren't really like that." The second servant doesn't try to convince the first servant that he already paid him back. Everyone just accepts on face value what they did wrong. When does that ever happen?

That doesn't mean anything is wrong with Jesus's parable. His point is that it is hypocritical for us Christians not to forgive in light of all we've been forgiven. That's true and we need to hear it. But too often we'll approach a parable like this as if Jesus was trying to give us the skills to manage the social strife that emerges when forgiveness is needed. We naively assume, if we were doing forgiveness right, then it would be as simple as the dialogues in this parable.

APPLYING BIBLICAL PARABLES

1. We make clear what the main point of the parable is. In this parable, the main point is that it is hypocritical to not forgive when we realize how much we've been forgiven. In the parable of the prodigal son (Luke 15), the main point is that after we've grown comfortable with our status of being forgiven, it is easy to become self-righteous toward those in need of forgiveness.

To use a parable for a purpose other than Jesus's purpose is to misuse it. Jesus chose the details of this parable to serve his main point. We wouldn't use the story of "Goldilocks and the Three Bears" to talk about woodworking, cooking techniques, or sleep strategies. Details about chair construction, porridge, and beds are in the story to help make the main point: Balance is better than extremes (i.e., too big, too small, just right; too hot, too cold, just right).

2. We acknowledge what tangential elements are oversimplified to focus on that main point. Parables leave out lots of important details for the purpose of highlighting the main point. Where were Goldilocks's parents? How did Goldilocks pick the lock on the bear's house? Did Smokey the Bear approve of the bear family having a fire in the forest to cook their porridge?

In the parable of the unforgiving servant, we would want to know the answers to many tangential questions if we were the pastor, counselor, or friend of one of the characters:

- Did the king ask for a business plan when he lent the money?
- Was the interest rate that caused the loan to get so high over an ethical rate?
- Did the first servant have a drug or gambling problem? How did he explain the growing debt?
- Was the first servant able to find a job to begin providing for his family?
- Did the second servant do something that hurt the first servant's business and caused the enormous debt?

- Who were the people who reported back to the king? Which servant were they better friends with?

Because this is a parable, there are no answers to these questions. These people never existed. They were figments of Jesus's imagination created to make a point about forgiveness.

But these kinds of questions are very relevant when we are seeking to help a friend think through how to navigate a broken relationship where forgiveness is needed.

3. We acknowledge that things tangential to a parable's point often are not tangential in life. It is easy to get so excited about Jesus's main point in a parable that we imply that Jesus's main point is the only point that needs to be made in any situation. But if that were the case, Jesus would not have needed to tell so many parables.

Perhaps we just ask our friend, "What details in your life don't seem to match up with the details of Jesus's parable?" Our friend might say, "The second servant acknowledged his debt and seemed to genuinely want to make it right. The person who hurt me won't acknowledge what they did and claims I'm wrong for even bringing it up." When we are teaching on a parable in a public setting, we need to think through these kinds of details.

Often our friend needs compassion toward the hardship surrounding their hurt as much as they need guidance on how to engage the person who offended them. Our compassion toward them is part of representing the Jesus whose parable we are trying to help them wisely apply.

4. We do not invoke biblical authority on speculations regarding things tangential in the parable. As we discover important questions not directly addressed in a parable, our friend (or audience) still needs guidance on those questions.

- We may find other biblical passages that speak directly to these questions.

- We may find biblical principles that help us discern the leading priorities that should guide decision-making.
- We may realize some important decisions are left free for the individual to decide based on conscience and preference.

The principle behind this fourth point is that, when we're talking about a parable, we want to avoid implying a given piece of advice has more biblical weight than it does. It is easy for someone to think that because a conversation or sermon began in a parable, that everything we say has the backing of biblical authority. With the parable we've been considering, common examples of this would be (a) equating a lingering sense of hurt or a struggle to trust with the hypocritical response of the unforgiving servant or (b) ignoring an assessment of resistance in the offending friend's response to acknowledging their sin as being relevant to how much the relationship is restored.

That means when we are talking with a hurt friend about this parable, we need to be willing to say things like, "Jesus's point in this parable is that you need to forgive. But what we've been talking about is what level of trust is warranted given how little your friend will own what they did. You being free from bitterness is one thing, but it doesn't mean you aren't hurt/frustrated by their resistance or that you need to put yourself in that position again. On those points, we're brainstorming together and looking for other relevant biblical principles and wise responses."

When we have conversations about forgiveness this way, we honor Jesus's intent for a parable, and we honor our friend as we help them learn to trust the Bible to guide their life through difficult, messy situations.

QUESTIONS FOR REFLECTION

1. How does this chapter help you interpret the Bible more accurately? If you enjoyed that part, you might also enjoy a book on hermeneutics (principles for interpreting the Bible) like *How*

to Read the Bible for All Its Worth by Gordon Fee and Douglas Stuart.

2. What are examples in your life (advice given to you or advice given by you) where a parable on forgiveness was used to give biblical weight to a point that wasn't the parable's main point? What was the effect of that error?

Chapter 25

WHEN DISCUSSING NARRATIVES INVOLVING FORGIVENESS

Parables are simpler than narratives. Parables are fictitious stories created to make a point. Narratives are the lived experiences of real people. Biblical narratives are the lived experiences of real people told to highlight an aspect of redemptive history (we'll come back to this point). In the previous chapter, we talked about using parables about forgiveness well. Now we need to consider how to use biblical narratives about forgiveness well.

Let's consider Joseph forgiving his brothers (Genesis 37–50), one of the most well-known biblical narratives about forgiveness. It involves great offenses: physical violence, lying, and human trafficking. It involves unexpected plot twists: a favorite son thought to be dead first becomes a slave and then vice president of Egypt before finally saving his family. It culminates with tears, embraces, and a memorable statement, "You meant evil against me, but God meant it for good, to bring it about that many people should be kept alive" (Genesis 50:20).

"That'll preach!" my country roots want to shout when we come to a crescendo statement like this. It is easy to land a sermon on

Joseph's life by answering these questions: If Joseph can forgive his brothers for all they did, what can't you forgive? If God saved Israel through Joseph's forgiveness, what might God do through yours?

"Amen! Good job! Preacher, you stepped all over my toes today!" Why do I keep alluding to my country roots? Hopefully, it makes you smile just a bit as we discuss the weighty subject of forgiveness. But more importantly, I want you to feel the weight of someone wanting to ask an honest question about biblical narratives on forgiveness. Our "amen" declarations stifle their "oh my" questions.

But real, important questions must be discussed if we want to be good ambassadors of how God intends forgiveness to be healing balm. We need to invite those questions. Our friend might want to ask:

- Would Joseph have responded to his brothers the same way if the power differentials[1] between them, which allowed his brothers to abuse him, had not been balanced?
- How much did Joseph being able to immediately see God's redemptive hand saving his family from the famine impact his response? How would Joseph's response have been different if his brothers came to him before the famine and before he became second-in-command to Pharaoh?
- Joseph had twenty years to process his brothers' request for forgiveness. What if this interaction had occurred much closer to their original ambush of Joseph?
- How often are we able to see clear redemptive elements in the fallout of other people's offenses? Does God always do that?
- Joseph's brothers were repentant and owned their sin. What if they still excused their actions based on their dad's

---

1. For more on the role of power differentials in this biblical narrative, see "The Story of Joseph: Abuse, Forgiveness, Power Differentials, and Wisdom," bradhambrick.com, November 5, 2019, http://bradhambrick.com/the-story-of-joseph-abuse-forgiveness-power-differentials-and-wisdom/.

preferential treatment or the offensiveness of Joseph's teenage ego? Would Joseph have fed them (grace) but not given them the restored rights of family members (reconciliation)?

- Joseph had a chance to test the character of his brothers before forgiving them (Genesis 44). What if he did not have this information when they asked his forgiveness?

I'll be honest with you. I don't know the answer to these questions. If we are going to be good ambassadors of the gospel, we must have the courage to engage questions we don't know the answer to. If we are only willing to consider questions that have certain answers, we will abandon those wrestling with the hardest situations.

APPLYING BIBLICAL NARRATIVES

So, in light of the bulleted list of questions, here are four points to consider on how to best use biblical narratives:

1. Celebrate the main point of the narrative and its place in redemptive history. Joseph's forgiveness is a beautiful picture of God's character. Joseph's words echo the later words of Jesus: "Father, forgive them, for they know not what they do" (Luke 23:34). Remember also that Jesus would be born from the family line preserved by Joseph's painful journey to Egypt. We see God orchestrating history in powerful ways through the worst of events.

These things should be highlighted and celebrated when discussing this narrative. When done so in harmony with the next three points, these truths are nourishing for everyone's soul—even those currently experiencing deep relational pain. When celebrated without awareness of these next three points, these truths can make God seem aloof and the gospel seem dangerous for the offended.

2. Consider the human person in a larger divine narrative. Often, we only use the experience of human characters in the Bible to emotionalize a story. We talk about pain, fear, despair, etc. But, when we get to the main point, we talk as if the redemptive elements (in this case, forgiveness) resolve all the emotional tensions.

We know our most biblical and gospel-rooted actions, like forgiveness, don't result in "happily ever after" lives. The world is too broken, and relationships are too complicated for that. If it's true now, it was true then (in biblical times). We need to teach the Bible as if we know this.

Joseph's brothers were probably jerks[2] again. Joseph likely still had nightmares about being beaten, thrown in a well, and sold as a slave. Joseph was a public figure during a famine; there had to be hard times, tough decisions, and people who disagreed with how Joseph cared for his family with Egyptian grain.

Asking questions like those in the bulleted list above allows people to grapple with the hard things in their life in light of the biblical narrative. All the details in Joseph's life may not line up with the details in their life. Applying the Bible well is not a matching quiz between biblical narrative and our current life events. It requires discernment to determine what principles are present or absent from a biblical narrative in order to arrive at how to apply the point of the text in our lives.

3. Remember that biblical narratives are written with hindsight. Moses wrote the Genesis account about Joseph. This means several generations' worth of perspective are included in the divine editorializing around Joseph's words in Genesis 50:20. We read the book of Genesis knowing the genealogy from Joseph saving his brothers led to Jesus (Matthew 1:1–17).

We don't make our decisions about forgiveness with hindsight. We try to apply these narratives midstory in our own lives. The book of the Bible that best captures our lived experience is

---

2. As we'll emphasize in the next chapter, it is important to note that in Genesis 37 Joseph's brothers were not just "jerks" but criminal human traffickers. At the stage in their life being discussed here, where Joseph was second-in-command to Pharaoh, "rude" was as bad as his brothers could be without severe legal repercussions.

Psalms, where the author is frequently writing with angst from the middle of a situation with an unknown outcome.

When we talk about Proverbs, we often, rightly, make the point that these are wisdom principles, not promises. God does not guarantee that a gentle answer will always turn away wrath (Proverbs 15:1), but it is wiser to be gentle than to make a volatile situation more explosive by responding in kind.

We should be willing to make a similar statement about biblical narratives, which are histories, not prescriptions. These are the real stories of real people who were a part of God's plan to bring a remedy to the problem of sin. These are not role plays where we memorize the lines of the character we most identify with and are guaranteed a comparable outcome.

4. Be prophetic on the main point and pastoral on the surrounding details. We have talked about how to interpret the Bible, but the point of this chapter is not primarily hermeneutics (i.e., principles of Bible interpretation). Rather we've been trying to learn how to effectively care for a hurting friend. Effective care for a friend does require that we interpret the Bible well. This final point is about balancing good Bible application with effective care for a friend.

The main point of a narrative about forgiveness tells us about God's ultimate agenda. It does not tell us the timetable in which that agenda will play out in our lives. The Bible tells the stories that were central to redemptive history. We learn about them with hindsight and divine commentary. About the main points we can say with the confident voice of a prophet, "See what God had done and trust God's character." We can proclaim these things with confidence.

Our friend makes choices about forgiveness midstory. We don't get hindsight and divine commentary on our lives. We learn about God's agenda of restoration and his power to restore from biblical narratives. We don't get a pacing guide, nor do we get an assessment of the repentance/safety of the person who harmed us. These are things we assess in order to make wise application of the teaching of Scripture and represent the character of God.

QUESTIONS FOR REFLECTION

1. What principle for understanding and applying biblical narratives stood out to you most from this chapter? What would be an example from a sermon, Bible study, or conversation with a friend where it would have made a big difference?
2. How does the reality that biblical narratives were written with hindsight and that we seek to apply them midstory impact how you apply these kinds of passages to your life?

Chapter 26

WHEN USING CRIMINAL OR TRAUMATIC OFFENSES AS ILLUSTRATIONS OF FORGIVENESS

Let's start this chapter by admitting that we like to use hyperbole—extreme examples to clarify our points. We Christians may be particularly fond of it when we're illustrating an important theme of the gospel, such as forgiveness.

Is hyperbole bad? No, Jesus used it (Matthew 5:27–30). Can it be used poorly? Yes. But before we get to the problem, let's consider the purpose of illustrations. We use illustrations to make points clearer. If illustrations don't make our point clearer, then they're not good illustrations—they're distractions. Sometimes this just results in ineffective teaching. Other times, it can be harmful to those being taught.

Imagine a father explaining forgiveness to his son. He uses the illustration of when his wife (the child's mother) forgave him for having an affair. The dad may be making theologically rich, well-articulated, and skillfully applied points about forgiveness.

But the illustration is a distraction. All the kid can think is, "Are my parents getting a divorce? Are we going to have to move?"

This is what we frequently do when we use criminal or traumatic offenses[1] as illustrations of what it means to forgive. When we recount the testimony of someone who has been raped, beaten, or similarly offended forgiving the person who abused them, we are putting every survivor who hears us in a comparable position as the son in the illustration above.

When, in a ministry context, we talk about someone forgiving their rapist, we are not providing legal or counseling advice on how to respond to the experience of rape. When we give an example of someone forgiving an abusive spouse or parent, we don't explain what happens when you call Child Protective Services (CPS) or how to make a safety plan.[2] But because survivors only hear their experience discussed in church as an illustration of forgiveness, they begin to think "just forgive" is the only guidance God has for them.

A good rule of thumb is don't use these kinds of illustrations if you do not have the training or time in your sermon/lesson to provide substantive guidance on how to respond to a criminal or traumatic experience. If we are going to use illustrations of this emotional weight, we must be willing to devote the time the subject matter requires. It is pastorally irresponsible to do otherwise.

ILLUSTRATIONS WITH CRIMINAL OFFENSES

When using an illustration or testimony involving a criminal offense, the following points would need to be made (this list is representative, not exhaustive):

---

1. Most offenses that are criminal are traumatic, but not every offense that is traumatic is criminal. What needs to be understood here is that criminality (legal process) and traumatic nature (healing process) of recovery from hurts of these kinds are different from normal day-to-day offenses.
2. For guidance on how to pastorally care in these situations, consider lessons 2, 3, 5, 6, and 7 at https://churchcares.com.

- It is right and God-honoring to report such an offense to the authorities (Romans 13), that is, the police.[3]
- If children or the elderly are being abused or neglected, it is mandatory to call CPS.
- If children are not involved and the thought of reporting is hard, it is wise for a survivor to talk to a counselor experienced in working with abuse/rape survivors because these are legitimately difficult decisions.
- Choosing to pursue legal action against criminal activity is not an expression of bitterness or unforgiveness.
- Forgiveness is one part, and usually not the first part, of the healing journey after the experience of abuse or rape.
- When you reach the point that forgiveness is the next part of God's healing process for you, forgiveness does not mean trusting or placing yourself in the position to be vulnerable again. If the person who hurt you demands trust or leverages the Bible against you, they are continuing to be abusive.

These points take time in a sermon or lesson. Admittedly, they steal the thunder from a point about forgiveness. But realize, without these clarifications, the "thunder" of your message will be haunting to someone who has not had the opportunity to process their experience.

ILLUSTRATIONS WITH TRAUMATIC EXPERIENCES

When using an illustration or testimony involving an offense that is traumatic, the following points would need to be made (this list is also representative, not exhaustive):

---

3. If you want to understand more about how Romans 13 and 1 Corinthians 6 harmonize with each other, consider reading "Why Is It Inappropriate (and Dangerous) to Alert an Alleged Offender of Abuse before Calling CPS and/or the Police?," bradhambrick.com, April 16, 2019, http://brad-hambrick.com/why-is-it-inappropriate-and-dangerous-to-alert-an-alleged-offender-of-abuse-before-calling-cps-and-or-the-police/.

- Painful memories are not the same thing as bitterness.
- Hypervigilance after a traumatic experience is not the same thing as a lack of faith.
- Flat emotions after a traumatic experience does not mean you're unloving, apathetic, or not worshipping.[4]
- Seeing a counselor experienced in working with trauma survivors can help a survivor learn to manage the emotional fluctuations that often occur after a trauma.
- Forgiveness does not erase memory. For offenses that are disruptive when remembered, Miroslav Volf's book *The End of Memory* can be a helpful discussion of forgiveness.

Again, these kinds of points do break the momentum of your sermon or lesson. But to the person who has experienced the kind of things you are using as an illustration, that "momentum" feels like an avalanche. To the person who is learning to manage their trauma, slower is safer. If we are going to speak of their life experience, then we should do so with the tenderness that experience requires.

This chapter forces us to consider again where we began this book—forgiveness means someone has been hurt. Criminal and traumatic offenses mean that there are more consequences to this person's pain.[5] We need to take this into account when we teach on or talk about forgiveness.

Considering these things, take a moment to read Psalm 23:1–4:

The LORD is my shepherd; I shall not want.
He makes me lie down in green pastures.

4. If you are unfamiliar with the common symptom clusters that frequently emerge after a traumatic experience, consider watching step 2 in this resource on trauma: "Post-Traumatic Stress (Seminar Videos)," bradhambrick.com, September 25, 2015, http://bradhambrick.com/ptsd/.
5. If you are prone to the rebuttal, "But aren't we all equally sinful? Criminal sin doesn't need to be double-dipped in the blood of Jesus, does it?" I encourage you to read "We Are Equally Sinful. We Are Not All Equally Broken or Toxic," bradhambrick.com, October 13, 2017, http://bradhambrick.com/we-are-equally-sinful-we-are-not-all-equally-broken-or-toxic/.

He leads me beside still waters.
    He restores my soul.
He leads me in paths of righteousness
    for his name's sake.

Even though I *walk* through the valley of the shadow of death,
    I will fear no evil,
for you are with me;
    your rod and your staff,
    they comfort me. (emphasis added)

Why did I choose to emphasize the word *walk*? It is a pacing verb. It reveals the pace at which the Good Shepherd is willing to go. The Good Shepherd moves at the pace that is best for the sheep. The scary setting—the valley of the shadow of death—does not rush the pace. The health and ability of the sheep set the pace. Sheep with a limp traverse the valley more slowly.

If we are going to be accurate ambassadors of the Good Shepherd, we must prioritize our ministry efforts the same way. We cannot let our zeal for the destination cause us to harm the sheep who have been entrusted to our care. That is what this chapter has been about: helping us pace our illustrations about forgiveness to the needs of those who have been hurt.

QUESTIONS FOR REFLECTION

1. When have you seen an illustration become a distraction? If it was around a sensitive subject, how did it detract from the care agenda of the person teaching?
2. How does the pacing verb "walk" of the Good Shepherd help you understand the pastoral significance in discussing criminal and traumatic offenses in the holistic manner recommended in this chapter?

Chapter 27

FORGIVENESS AND THE ASSURANCE OF SALVATION: RELIGIOUS SCRUPULOSITY

You may see the phrase "religious scrupulosity" and think, "Scrabble jackpot!" But for those who experience an unrelenting and irrational preoccupation with guilt, this struggle is life-altering. Admittedly, this chapter is more technical than other chapters in this book. But if we are going to minister well on the subject of forgiveness, we need to understand how the experience of common guilt is different from religious scrupulosity.

Religious scrupulosity is defined as a "pathological guilt about moral or religious issues. It is personally distressing, objectively dysfunctional, and often accompanied by significant impairment in social functioning. It is typically conceptualized as a moral or religious form of obsessive-compulsive disorder (OCD)."[1] We will need to take a moment to unpack that definition.

In the same way that individuals who experience OCD can fixate on germs, locked doors, the oven being turned off, or doing

---

1. This description is taken from "Scrupulosity," wikipedia.org, last edited February 3, 2021, 22:13 https://en.wikipedia.org/wiki/Scrupulosity.

tasks in even or odd sets, OCD can fixate on the assurance of salvation. An obsession is the cognitive fixation on a perceived problem, and a compulsion is a ritual believed to remedy the problem.

For religious scrupulosity, the obsessions might include one or more of the following:

- fixation that one hasn't been religious enough or must practice their faith perfectly
- fears that one is saying their prayers incorrectly or parts have been left out
- unrelenting fears of having committed the unforgivable sin or having blasphemed the Holy Spirit
- repeated thoughts of saying something blasphemous during prayer or at church
- intrusive thoughts (including sexual thoughts) about religious figures or God

For religious scrupulosity, the compulsions might include:

- continually asking for God's forgiveness
- constantly mulling over one's words or actions, wondering if the words have double meanings of a sacrilegious or blasphemous nature or if their behavior was sinful
- praying or performing religious rituals for hours to ensure that rituals are performed perfectly
- saying prayers a certain number of times, perhaps a number with biblical significance
- repeatedly asking pastors and other church leaders the same question to be sure they understand the answer completely[2]

---

2. These lists of obsessions and compulsions are modified and adapted from "Recognizing and Counseling People Who Have Scrupulosity," beyondocd.org, https://beyondocd.org/information-for-clergy/recognizing-and-counseling-people-who-have-scrupulosity.

A SPIRITUAL AND PHYSICAL BATTLE

Perhaps you know someone who struggles in this way and have seen your friend be debilitated socially, emotionally, and spiritually. If so, you are likely asking, "What value is gained by placing this kind of struggle in the category of OCD?" We will consider three advantages that emerge.

1. We realize we are facing a neurological challenge, not just a cognition (belief) problem. Brain scans for individuals who experience OCD show key differences from those who do not. Physician and biblical counselor Michael Emlet has reviewed the medical literature and encouraged Christians to recognize this reality.[3]

This recognition allows for a both-and approach, and it can help alleviate some of the guilt that is so central to the experience of religious scrupulosity. For a parallel example, consider the person who believes they are struggling with the sin of sloth (i.e., laziness). But they later learn they have anemia (i.e., a low red blood cell count that has left them feeling weak and fatigued). This medical finding doesn't erase the problem of low activity. It provides an additional means of addressing the problem.

Our friend with anemia could still say, "I believe I would honor God and enjoy life more if I were more active." Our friend would still be responsible for taking the steps necessary to move in this direction. However, these steps would include a high-iron diet and other medical interventions, not only repentance and faith-based actions. Our friend could engage the medical helps with faith and gratitude to God for allowing science to help us understand how these things impact their struggle.

2. We see more clearly the need to expand the helping team. Having a skilled Christian psychiatrist or counselor experienced with OCD becomes a natural step to take. Professional counselors

---

3. For a brief (only thirty-two pages), readable summary of Dr. Emlet's work in this area, see the minibook *OCD: Freedom for the Obsessive-Compulsive* (Phillipsburg, NJ: P&R Publishing, 2003), which contains both his assessment of the medical literature and guidance for pastoral care and counseling.

do not replace pastoral care, but it ensures that each helper is doing what they do best.[4]

Pastorally, working with a psychiatrist helps the person struggling with religious scrupulosity make necessary distinctions.

- If a pastor tries to address this struggle on their own, the pastor is inadvertently reinforcing the belief that this struggle is exclusively spiritual.
- If a pastor just refers and doesn't remain engaged for pastoral care, they communicate that the problem is only physical.

We want to embody, not only advise, a both-and approach. That takes us to the question, "What does pastoral care look like in this kind of situation?"

3. *We identify the kind of care strategies that are most helpful for our friend.* We realize that it is not productive to try to explain key biblical texts that frequently become the focal point of individuals experiencing religious scrupulosity (e.g., Matthew 12:30–32; Hebrews 6:4–6). This is like taking someone to nursing school whose OCD fixates on germ contamination. It seems like it might be helpful, but when we realize the fear being battled is irrational, we quit trying to use education to remedy this fear.

We want our friend to doubt their fear enough to turn their attention to something else. Imagine our friend as a wild animal caught in a net. The more they fight against the net, the tighter the net gets. If we wanted to help them, what is the first thing we would ask them to do? Relax and quit fighting, so the net can be loosened. What is the religious scrupulosity equivalent of relaxing? Doubting the fear.

---

4. For more guidance on how pastoral care and professional counseling can supplement each other well, see the fifteen-minute video "The Pastor as Counselor Lesson 7: Mental Health and Pastoral Care," Pastor as Counselor series, bradhambrick.com, February 18, 2020, http://bradhambrick.com/pastorascounselor7/.

How do we help our friend doubt their fear? We help them see the pattern, not just the event. OCD is a pattern consisting of obsessive thoughts and compulsive rituals. Every pattern is a series of events. But the more our friend fixates on a particular event—a troublesome thought or corresponding behavior—the more they despair.

Consider another analogy. OCD is a washing machine spinning too fast. Now, imagine the question about the assurance of salvation is a shoe in that washing machine. It makes an awful noise. No one in the house can focus on anything else. If you wanted to get the shoe out, what is the first thing you would do? You would slow the spin cycle. If you reached in while it was spinning full speed, your arm would get beat up and you would be unable to retrieve the shoe. Slowing the machine down is a picture of the strategy of doubting our fears.

The conversation might sound something like this:

"You have proven you are willing to do whatever God asks. Your desire to honor God is exceptional; actually, it's so strong it's becoming debilitating. Over the years, how many actions or thoughts have you feared would cost you your salvation? All I am asking is that you consider that the pattern of thought—fixating on losing your salvation—may be the real problem. If so, a loving God—one worth devoting your life to—would want you to stop torturing yourself."

After conversations like this, you will likely have to help your friend realize you are not minimizing their sin. Instead, you are emphasizing the character of the God who delights in redeeming and freeing his children from sin and any other bondage that impedes their ability to enjoy the full life God intends for them. From there, the goal becomes engagement in any God-honoring activity your friend enjoys.

QUESTIONS FOR REFLECTION

1. Review the list of obsessions and compulsions frequently associated with religious scrupulosity. How are these different from normal conviction and legitimate concern for the condition of one's soul?

2. Imagine a friend who is irrationally doubting their salvation, to such a degree that it is impairing their life functioning. How would you, in your own words, have a version of the "doubt your fears" conversation like the vignette above?

Conclusion

THE NEXT CHAPTER
OF YOUR LIFE

I hope this book has felt like a good friend in hard times. If so, getting to the end of this book may feel a bit like grief. That is how the conclusion of many good growth processes feel. We are glad to be in a better place, but we will miss the people and resources God used in the journey.

Something that is often overlooked about grief is that the grieving are the ones whose story continues. While this book has reached its last chapter, your life has many chapters yet to be written.

In *grief-by-death*, this transition is sad. We lament embracing the next chapter without our loved one. In *grief-by-growth*, this transition is a compliment and celebration of the hard work you have done. You have persevered through the difficult terrain of forgiveness. You have mustered the courage to be vulnerable in healthy relationships. You have sought to discern what wise trust looks like in relationships that were broken. You have come a long way.

At this stage in your journey, I want you to hear me say two things to you: "*Thank you* for allowing me to be a companion on this journey; it has been an honor," and "*Well done*. Forgiveness is like a marathon; there is great merit in finishing, regardless of how long it takes." Take a moment. Look in the mirror. Smile. Even if, metaphorically speaking, your face is tired and dirty, take satisfaction that this is the sweat of a well-run race.

The question before you now is, "What's next?" Don't rush to answer this question. If you need to rest, then rest. But this book has been about finding freedom—freedom from the emotional weight of needing to forgive or embracing forgiveness. Now you get to answer the exciting question, "Freedom to do *what*?" We do the work to obtain emotional freedom to be able to invest that freedom in something. What is that something for you?

Here are nine questions meant to help you discern what God has for you next.

1. Am I willing to commit my life to whatever God asks of me? This is a "do not pass go" question. If your answer is "no," it likely means you still need to rest and recover from the work you've just done. Remember, Sabbath was God's idea. He's in favor of it. Do not get lost in guilt or pretend that your answer is "yes." You've been too honest about life and its challenges for that. Rather, identify the obstacle and engage with it.

Are there specific things you believe God is asking of you? Be sure to record your thoughts on this question before reflecting on the subsequent questions.

2. What roles has God placed me in? The first part of being a good steward of your life is to fulfill your primary roles with excellence. When Paul says in Ephesians 5:17 that we are to "understand what the will of the Lord is," he goes on to describe God's design for major life roles (spouse, parent, child, and worker in 5:22–6:9).

3. What are my spiritual gifts? Stewarding your life involves utilizing the spiritual gifts God has given you. God gives spiritual gifts that coincide with the calling he places on each of our lives. Read Romans 12:1–8 and 1 Corinthians 12:1–30 for a list of these gifts. Which are evident in your life? If you need further assistance discerning this, talk to your pastor about taking a spiritual gifts inventory.

4. For what group of people (age, struggle, career, nation, language, etc.) am I burdened? From God's earliest covenant with people, his intention was to bless us that we might be a blessing to others (Genesis 12:2). Investing your life in those you have a burden for allows you to be other-minded and find joy in it.

5. What am I passionate about? At this point, you can begin to see Psalm 37:3–8 fulfilled in your life. What are the God-exalting "delights" in your life (v. 4)? What wholesome things can you give yourself to and you are more energized afterward?

6. With what talents or abilities has God blessed me? These don't have to be spiritual gifts. Read the amazing description of "ordinary but exceptional" abilities God gave Bezalel and how he used those abilities to serve God (Exodus 31:1–11). Think through the skills and expertise you have accumulated in your life.

7. What are my unique life experiences? Both pleasant and unpleasant experiences should be listed. We are sometimes tempted to think that God can only use the good or spiritual experiences of our lives. God is glad to use our successes (Matthew 5:16), but God also delights in displaying his grace by transforming our low points for his glory (2 Corinthians 1:3–5).

8. Where do my talents and passions match up with the needs in my church and community? We should seek to steward our lives in cooperation with our local church. God's way of blessing and maturing those we serve is through the body of Christ, the church. By identifying where your gifts, burdens, passions, and abilities fit within or expand your church's ministries, you are maximizing the impact your service can have on those you are seeking to bless.

9. How would God have me bring these things together to glorify him? This is not a new question but a summary question. Look back over what you have written in response to the first eight questions. Talk about it with your Christian friends, family, mentor, or pastors. Ask God to give you a sense of direction. Then begin serving as a way to steward your life for God's glory.